Literacy Learning in the Early Years
THROUGH CHILDREN'S EYES

Literacy Learning in the Early Years
THROUGH CHILDREN'S EYES

Linda Gibson

CASSELL

Cassell Educational Limited
Artillery House
Artillery Row
London SW1P 1RT

First published in 1989

British Library Cataloguing-in-Publication Data

Gibson, Linda
   Literacy learning in the early years: Through children's eyes.
   1. Pre-school children. Reading skills. Acquisition
   I. Title
   372.4

ISBN 0-304-31873-6

Typeset by Graphic Composition, 240 Hawthorne Avenue, Athens, Georgia 30606

Printed in U.S.A.

Contents

Acknowledgments

I began my career in education as a graduate student at the Bank Street College of Education. I had come to New York City with a liberal arts degree, which I quickly discovered prepared me for very little in the way of work. Becoming a teacher had never been at the top of my list of career choices. Like most of the population, I tended to believe that the early years of education were not especially important. Early schooling, as I remembered it, consisted of activities that had predetermined ends and that had as a central goal teaching children how to follow directions. Mostly, I recall being very bored in my first years in school. But my Bank Street College experience produced a definitive shift in my limited views of early education. Becoming a member of that unique and wonderful community of educators was the beginning of a very rewarding career.

My first job was as an assistant teacher to Louise Crowe. We taught four-year-olds at the Downtown Community School in New York City. The director of the nursery–kindergarten program, Irene Neurath, provided leadership for a thoughtful and dedicated group of early childhood educators committed to the exploration of a humanistic approach to education. At our weekly faculty meetings, we discussed our programs from the point of view of not just what we did, but, more important, why we did what we did. Nothing was taken for granted. We scrutinized every aspect of our programs until we had unearthed the thread that led from theory to practice and back again.

I remember how I would come away from our meetings unable to pinpoint a specific activity that I might add to my program. But as weeks or even years went by, I found I would return to the perspective on teaching and learning that had been so clearly articulated in these sessions. The intersection of children, program, and teacher was a dynamic one, a meeting in which the idea of teachers learning from children was as critical as that of children learning about the world.

Eventually, Irene and our team of N–K teachers began the Corlears School, also in New York City. We decided to expand our program and to add a grade each year through the middle elementary years. The expansion had a specific goal: to bring our well-established teaching approach, rooted in the integration of principles of child development with classroom programs, to elementary classrooms. Irene invited Dr. Frances Minor of New York University to be our consultant and to help us in the task of reforming the traditional elementary program. In many lively faculty meetings, Frances challenged us to reflect upon and articulate a basic theoretical framework around which to build an elementary program that emphasized the integration of subject areas. Never prescriptive in her approach, Frances set in motion a way of thinking about teaching and learning which has stayed with me and which I continue to use as a guide in my teaching and writing.

In recent years, Marion Greenwood has become the director of Corlears. I have continued my relationship with the school as a language consultant and as a partner in some of the teacher-research projects. This year I had the opportunity to do a series of videotapes of two classes of three-year-olds, one of which was taught by Louise Crowe. I continue to learn so much from Louise, whose storytime sessions are the focus of one of the chapters in this book.

In my work at Queens College, I have had the unique opportunity to supervise the field work of undergraduate students at P.S. 148 in the borough of Queens in New York City. It is here that I have witnessed the beginnings of a collaborative educational community within the public school system. The perspectives of teaching and learning so firmly impressed upon me in my years at Bank Street and Corlears have been realized in this school setting. Sal Romano, the principal, and Laurie Pessah, the writing process coordinator in the district, have fostered the development of a school community in which teachers are encouraged and supported as innovators and designers of their reading and writing programs. Diane Epstein, Patti Golombas, Elaine Iodice, Nivia Alvarez, Diane Sohl, and Debbie Futerman are some of the teachers from whom my student advisees and I have learned to design and implement whole language programs.

A key influence in the growth of the innovative classrooms at P.S. 148 and at many other schools in the city is the "Teachers College Writing Project," directed by Lucy Calkins. Though the attempt to transform the New York City public school system presents some enormous problems, it also presents unusual challenges to those who are persistent and dedicated in their efforts to bring about change. Lucy Calkins and her team of teacher educators are among those who have made such a commitment and who have, as a result, made a difference in elementary education in New York City.

I am grateful to friends and colleagues who have read and critiqued passages of this manuscript as it has evolved. William Profriedt, whose writing and whose talent for writing have been a source of inspiration, broadened my approach to parts of the manuscript. Marcia Baghban not only gave me critical feedback and advice on first drafts of most of the chapters, but her book (Baghban, 1984), which describes her study of her daughter's literacy development from birth to three, provided an original inspiration for this book. My understanding of early stages of literacy learning has been definitively shaped by her writing and by our discussions. The Queens College administration granted me release time (Faculty in Residence Award, 1987–88), which eased the burden of completing the writing of the manuscript. Finally, I was blessed with a wonderful developmental editor, Susan Liddicoat of Teachers College Press, who cheerfully read and reread drafts of this manuscript, and who helped me to keep the overall structure and organization of the book clearly in focus.

Introduction

It was a snowy morning in February, and I couldn't take my class of three-year-olds outside. Instead, I took the group to the indoor gym for playtime. Some folding chairs with desk-type arms had been left there from a parent meeting the night before. Becca, one of my more precocious youngsters, was immediately intrigued. She lined the chairs up so that they faced one direction. She corralled enough children to fill the seats, stood in front of the group, and announced that she was the teacher. She passed out paper and pencils and proceeded to instruct her students by telling them letters they should write. And her students more or less followed her instructions.

I watched this scene unfold in amazement. Where, I kept asking myself, did Becca get her vision of such a classroom? For most of these youngsters, their first school experience was in my room, a program that did not resemble the one they were reenacting. Becca had a ten-year-old sister who was a student in the same school, but, although the program was more structured for older children, her sister's classroom was not a model for the one she was re-creating. As a teacher, Becca adopted the personality of the benevolent authority—she had an inviting manner, but she was the boss.

The children's social drama didn't last very long—except in my own mind where I returned to it again and again. The idea of the formal classroom community, what it looks like and how it is structured, is communicated very quickly in our society. Becca had never been a member of such a class group; nevertheless she possessed a rudimentary understanding of what it was like. *Teacher-centered* is the label commonly used to describe the highly structured organization of the social and academic programs in elementary classrooms.

Moreover, Becca seemed to have grasped the idea that teaching reading—something that she interpreted as having to do with writing letters—is a major part of what goes on in a typical classroom. Indeed, learning to read, a central focus of the elementary program since its nineteenth-century beginnings, continues to be the major focus of current programs. And time-honored formal teaching methods for the early grades—the concentrated focus on phonic skills and word identification—describe, in large part, contemporary approaches. The impact of these programs, especially on young-sters in the primary grades, is problematic. Those who learn to read appear to do so in spite of, rather than because of, these programs. Briefly, the prob-lem is that these items of information about print forms are isolated from the main premise of language use, whether spoken or written, which is the com-munication of meaning.

An analogous approach to teaching youngsters to speak would be to drill them on the pronunciation of speech sounds and to curtail talk until the articulation of the sounds has been mastered. Undoubtedly, such an approach would hinder, if not entirely inhibit, the development of speech. There would be many youngsters, however, who would survive the experience, by ignor-ing the program and by learning from their experiences outside the teaching situation.

It is only relatively recently that literacy learning has become a deliberate focus of the nursery and kindergarten curriculum. The thrust of these pro-grams, rather than interweaving with the traditionally child-centered, infor-mal teaching methods of N–K classes, has been to take formal materials and approaches used in the grades and to transform them for younger children. The problems with the formal approach to teaching reading in the early grades are magnified when transferred to N–K programs. Over the past cen-tury, the accumulation of research in child development, including language acquisition, states unequivocally that learning experiences for young chil-dren (including the primary ages) must be active in nature. Literacy learning, especially, is an active process in which children reconstruct for themselves the rules of the system through participation in meaningful acts of reading and writing. Teaching materials that separate literacy learning from the com-munication of meaning are confusing and even intimidating to youngsters who don't already have a good grasp of what reading is and how it is accom-plished.

The major focus of this book is to suggest ways for bringing greater con-gruence between literacy teaching and literacy learning. I am especially con-cerned with the impact that current teaching trends have upon the youngest members of the school community, those in the kindergartens and the early grades. The understanding of how to design literacy programs for these years must be derived from our understanding of the roots of language learning, of which literacy learning is a part. The largely successful, informal teaching methods of the home, highlighted by the fact that nearly all youngsters learn to talk, need to be considered as one of our best guides for the design of school programs.

In this book, the descriptions of literacy learning for the birth-through-eight age range are organized in chronological order. Reading and writing behaviors common to each age are provided. Part I describes interactions between children and caregivers that are especially significant to language learning. Home to school connections are described in Part II within the context of model language and literacy programs for three-year-olds. In Part III, selected descriptions of N–K classes provide guidelines for the design of literacy programs for these ages. The last part addresses problems with traditional reading and writing programs for the primary grades and proposes alternative approaches.

Chronology, however, should never be applied as the sole measure of what children should be doing at any point in time. Chronological growth only loosely describes the sequence of literacy learning. The pace and integration of acquisition are determined by the individual youngster. The outstanding feature of the child's relationship to all areas of language learning is that it is developmental in nature. Beginning efforts to speak, read, and write are significantly different from later expressions. Early behaviors, however, form the foundation for the evolution of later behaviors.

A major premise underlying descriptions of educational moments in this book is that teaching and learning are related experiences. In this view, educational events are understood as transactional: Teaching and learning are experienced by both teacher and learner. Teachers must continually ask themselves what it is the learner is gaining from their teaching. Learners, on the other hand, need opportunities to play back, or teach, what they have gained from their experiences.

Also, though I rely on the familiar labels of "reading" and "writing" to organize much of the material in this book, I do not mean to imply that these experiences are separated in either the act of teaching or that of learning. The phrase "literacy learning" is meant to underscore the connections between these two sides of the written language coin. Encounters with written language are unified in the sense that they engage learners in the process of constructing meanings—either those proposed by another or those that they want to communicate. The labels, however, represent a useful way to describe the different behaviors children exhibit in relation to each of these categories as well as the different actions teachers might take in shaping programs in which children are invited to construct meanings via written language.

The descriptions of authentic classroom experiences which fill each chapter provide portraits of some of the teachers and children whom I have taught and from whom I have learned. I have tried to present the educational experience as a partnership between adults and children. My hope is that these scenes will inspire teachers to rethink what they do and how they do it, especially in relation to the design of their language programs.

Part I

BIRTH THROUGH TWO

1

Learning to Speak

When asked how children learn to speak, nearly all of the students in my college classes respond with some variation of the imitation theory. Babies, they reason, are regularly spoken to by their mothers or caregivers during the first year. Hence at the beginning of the second year, they are ready to begin on their own. I suggest that a logical extension of this idea would be for the infant's first utterances to go something like this: "Hi, Mom, I'm having such a good time in my crib. Will you come play with me?" This would, after all, be a relatively close imitation of the talk that the child has been exposed to during the first year. Students protest that, of course, this is not what they mean, that babies begin with "baby talk"—babbling that turns into words. With more probing on my part, students expand the imitation theory to include other common conceptions about infant learning. Through the regular association of things and their names and the use of parental reinforcement—"Right, dear, *doggie,* that's a doggie"—the child slowly becomes a full-fledged member of the language community. And, students claim, it is the constant repetition of these labeling episodes that accounts for children's language learning. Though these views are not entirely mistaken, they do not account for key aspects of the development of child speech.

At this point I introduce an example of rule invention. One of my favorite samples was recorded by Jean Berko-Gleason (1967) in conversation with a four-year-old girl.

CHILD: My teacher holded the baby rabbits and we patted them.
JBG: Did you say your teacher held the baby rabbits?
CHILD: Yes.
JBG: What did you say she did?
CHILD: She holded the baby rabbits and we patted them.
JBG: Did you say she held them tightly?
CHILD: No, she holded them loosely.

First, though the child clearly understood what was being asked and was twice exposed to the past tense of *hold,* she did not imitate the adult. Even

3

more interesting is the child's invented past tense for *hold,* the use of *ed,* which is the regular marker for past tense. Though the child clearly has not been exposed to *holded* in the language community around her, the impulse to stick with the rules as she currently understands them is very strong. It is at this point that there begins to be a breakthrough in the discussion with the teachers-to-be. As they examine the episode and begin to reflect upon the child's ingenious efforts, a different perspective of the language learning task begins to take shape. Most, in fact, can come up with their own samples of rule or word invention that they remember hearing from young children.

What begins to penetrate is that the process is more complex than had previously been thought and that the ingenious efforts of young children in deriving and applying the rules of the system are not to be underestimated. Adult resistance to the idea that learning to speak is a complicated task can be traced to the fact that the process takes place without any formal instruction. How, they ask, can small children manage to move ahead with so little explicit guidance? Even the most disbelieving admit that rule explanations— "No, dear, *hold* has an irregular past tense; it doesn't use *ed*"—will not in any way aid the preschooler in coming to grips with language forms. In fact, all agree such abstract reasoning with a small child would be very inhibiting and out of place. In order to gain an understanding of the origins of this remarkable learning process, it is necessary to begin with the child's first year and to examine what goes on in the infant's life during those months that precede the coming of the first words.

THE FIRST YEAR

During a warm afternoon in June, I heard my neighbor and her three-month-old, Michael, "talking" to each other on their patio. Michael was in his carriage and had just awakened from a nap. As he began to "coo" and "ahhh," his mother began to echo his sounds. As Michael's sounds went up and down the scale, so did his mother's. After a few minutes, Michael's cooing turned into crying and what his mother interpreted as a demand to be fed. At that point she took him inside for the feeding.

In Gordon Wells' excellent book *The Meaning Makers* (1986), the significance of such exchanges between infant and caregiver, familiar to anyone who has spent even a short time around babies, is carefully documented. What Wells makes clear is that the infant's apparently effortless entry into the world of communication around age one has some identifiable precursors in the first months of life.

First, infants are born with a drive to make sense of their surroundings. Not the passive creatures they appear to be, infants are taking in what goes on around them; they are looking for explanations for phenomena and making predictions about their experiences. One experiment, quoted by Wells (1986), reveals that at five months "infants are able to track a moving object behind a screen, anticipate its emergence at the other side, and show surprise if a different object appears" (p. 34). Most of us, moreover, have watched an older infant delight in repeatedly dropping an object out of the crib or from the highchair in order to have someone retrieve it. Such actions indicate that youngsters have already learned something about manipulating their environment.

Moreover, infants possess a natural sociability. "Babies show a clear preference for faces and face-like shapes and show that they distinguish human voices from other sounds" (Wells, 1986, p. 34). Infants tend to orient themselves to important adults in a way that is appealing and satisfying for both. It is this cooing and babbling of mothers and infants that sets the basis for communication. The wordless "conversation"—the kind between Michael and his mother—is carried on through taking turns and by each giving the other full attention.

> In this relationship [infants] also learn to take a more active part in controlling the sequencing of turns that make up an interaction and discover the contingent nature of the relationship between turns, as they notice how their own specific behavior regularly elicits particular types of behavior from their partners, and they begin to produce particular types of behavior themselves in response to specific behavior by others. (Wells, 1986, p. 35)

The highly sophisticated cueing between conversational partners grows out of this early introduction to turn-taking in the wordless, but expressive, dialogues between infants and caretakers.

Further, because of the repetitive quality of the infant's experiences in the first months, there is ample opportunity to make connections among people, events, and things. The cycle of experiences that fill the infant's day is sleeping, eating, dressing, and bathing. Each of these events generally takes place in the same location and involves the same people and objects. At six months or before, infants begin to reach for the bottle when it appears at feeding time. Upon seeing the pacifier, they will ready their mouth to receive it.

During these daily episodes of bathing, dressing, and so forth, the caregivers, when not engaged in wordless conversations with their charges, often talk to the infants about what is happening. "Oh, look, there's the rubber duck!" can be a usual accompaniment to bath time; "Now we're going to put on the blue pajamas" is commonly heard at bedtime. For the baby's benefit, these monologues are most often delivered in the playful-sounding modulations of pitch and tone characteristic of cooing. In this way parents provide a network of talk that connects them to their infants and ties both to descriptions of the event. In these early months, language often functions as an accompaniment to the activity at hand.

Finally, a key aspect in this process is the caregiver's mediating of the infant's intentions. Right from birth, parents tend to find meaning in the infant's vocalizations. Just as Michael's mother interpreted his cooing-turned-to-crying as an indication of hunger, so other cries are interpreted as the infant's ways of signaling other meanings.

It is the process of identifying intentions that is significant in the language learning process. Given the context of the situation, the caregiver's constant contact with the infant, and the limited number of events in the child's daily routine, infant desires and adult interpretations are bound to be congruent most of the time. It is interesting to note, though, that regardless of whether there is a meeting of the minds, so to speak, the adults are signaling the infant that communication is designed to carry meaning or intentions. As Wells (1986) puts it, "By being treated *as if* they already had intentions, babies do in time come to have them, discovering in the process that their behavior can affect the people in their environment—that they can indeed communicate" (p. 35). Thus, through daily actions and interpretations of gestures and vocalizations, Michael's mother will introduce him to the categories of meaning that have significance for her and, by extension, to the community into which Michael has been born. Before the end of his first year—before uttering his first word—Michael is coming to understand key aspects of communication. What Wells describes is known as the social interactionist theory of language learning. As the name suggests, this view holds that it is the nature of the interaction between infants and caregivers that provides the key to language development. As described, the infant arrives with particular endowments which, combined with adult responses, support the child's relatively effortless entry into the world of speech.

THE LEARNING PROCESS

Jerome Bruner (1983), whose research in the development of speech has been extremely illuminating, uses playtimes, a favorite way of interacting between infants and caregivers, as a model of children's learning processes. Certain games seem to find favor with generation after generation of English-speaking parents and children. "Ride-a-cock-horse" is one of these (baby is rhythmically bounced as parent repeats rhyme), as is "Pat-a-cake-pat-a-cake-bakers-man" (finger and hand play accompanies the repeating of the rhyme).

Another favorite is "peek-a-boo." It was the playing of this game by Jonathan and his mother that Bruner (1983) recorded over a period of 10 months. The recording of the play episodes began when Jonathan was two months old. At that point, the game consisted of the mother hiding either her own face or Jonathan's and repeating "peek-a-boo" when the hidden face was exposed. When Jonathan was five months old, a new version was introduced in which a toy clown was hidden in a cone and then popped out through the manipulation of the stick to which it was attached. Initially the sequence of the game consisted of first getting Jonathan's attention ("Jonathan, see what I have"). The mother then had the clown disappear ("He's gone. Where is he?"), which was followed by the reappearance of the clown ("He's coming. Look, Jonathan! Here he is.") (p. 51).

Bruner points out that though the game actions always followed the same sequence, the parts were continually varied. Suspense was engendered by the mother's variations in timing (actions could be slow or explosive) and voice intonation. Jonathan's response to the game was, first, to grab the clown (five months); then, to grab while vocalizing (six months); and, by eight months, to indicate he was no longer content to be merely a spectator. At that point, his actions indicated he wanted to get the clown up and out of the cone himself. As a result, in order to keep his attention, his mother allowed him to become a co-participant in the game.

In his ninth and tenth months, Jonathan lost interest in the clown game. It was replaced by variations on the peek-a-boo theme. His mother used a toy hidden behind her back as the game format. Or, she hid herself behind a chair and then reappeared on cue, responding with the predictable, "boo." In his twelfth month, Jonathan became the initiator of this game by hiding himself behind a chair and then reappearing with his version of "boo" ("ooo").

The last phase that Bruner documented was the reappearance of the clown game when Jonathan was 14 months old. At this point he could participate as either initiator or spectator.

> He preferred the more active role but did not monopolize it. He played it rather well; first ejecting the clown from its cone while vocalizing his variant of *boo!* (*ooo!*), then approximating his mother's *all gone* (*a ga*) while stuffing the clown back into its cone. Finally he imitated his mother's *peekaboo* with *pick* as he yanked the clown out again and again stuffed it back. (p. 55)

The developments in the game frame highlight the nature of the teaching/learning process in which Jonathan and his mother were co-participants. First, over the course of the year, Jonathan learned a great deal about negotiating the interaction or, put simply, about taking turns by "moving from the grabbiness of the six-month-old to the highly tuned participation of the [one] year-old" (Bruner, 1983, p. 55). Second, Jonathan correctly incorporated the verbal accompaniments to the game. Bruner points out that this accomplishment has as much to do with learning about cultural conventions—in this case the format of the game—as it does with language learning.

Finally, of utmost importance is the mother's role in slowly handing the game over to Jonathan. Bruner dubs this the "handover principle" and emphasizes the ubiquitousness of this process in the early talk and play of infants and caregivers. "If," Bruner writes, "the 'teacher' in such a system were to have a motto, it would surely be 'where before there was a spectator, let there now be a participant'" (p. 60). This kind of turn-taking and attunement of mother to child has been called "scaffolding." The process is one in which the adult sets up "the situation to make the child's entry easy and successful and then gradually [pulls] back and [hands] the role to the child as he becomes skillful enough to manage it" (p. 60).

The significance of these collaborative efforts cannot be underestimated. As Bruner points out, it is central to all major learning jointly undertaken by adult and child as the former inducts the latter into the cultural community in which they both live. The game situation just described represents one format in which patterns of exchange are shaped by clearly defined roles that become reversible. While the adult is able to fine tune his or her responses to the child in order to make this response possible, the child, after much priming, is capable of picking up and reacting appropriately to the clues. Initially, the infant adopts a passive role and simply reacts to the mother's playful prompting. In time, though, as Jonathan demonstrates, the child becomes the initiator and/or leader in beginning and continuing the game.

THE FIRST WORDS

The kind of fine tuning that the infant brings to the game situation is extended to other interactions with adults. Not a creature tied solely to experiences in the here-and-now, the child is capable of generalizing the ability to collaborate from one situation to another. Language learning represents a prime example of this ability. Accompanying game playing are exchanges between caregivers and infants that are directly concerned with naming familiar objects and people in the child's circumscribed world. Bruner (1983) describes the quality of this interaction between baby Jonathan, beginning at age three months, and his mother. The mother holds a familiar object between herself and Jonathan while the two of them are looking at each other.

As she does so, she changes her expression to a characteristic and standard form: "See the pretty dolly" [her rising intonation stresses "dolly"]. . . . She characteristically accompanied the vocalization by moving the object into the child's line of regard and shaking or otherwise "forefronting" it. (p. 71)

These kinds of episodes between adults and infants are repeated many times during the first year, using familiar objects. In order to signal to Jonathan that they were going to participate in one of these naming sessions, his mother would say his name with a rise in pitch and stress in the middle of the name, as an attention getter. By five months, Jonathan regularly responded to the repetition of his name in this fashion. He would either look toward his mother or look for the thing his mother was looking at.

Similar to the game format, infants become more active in taking on the role of highlighting familiar people and objects, as these naming episodes accumulate. On their way to using words, pointing becomes a standard method for the one-year-old to call attention to something. Babies also invent their own vocalizations. One twelve-month-old was recorded as using "aaaaa" to express pleasure and "eeee" for protest (Dore, Franklin, Miller, & Ramer, 1976). These types of expressions are called vocables and are defined as regular sound patterns unique to an individual child and used in consistent situations.

Characteristically, the first words are loose approximations of adult speech. As noted, Jonathan pronounced *boo* as "ooo." At other times, he pronounced *apple* as "apoo" and *bird* as "bue." What is significant is that the child begins to use these truncated but recognizable words in ways that are appropriate and consistent. At this point, children are simply adding words as another way of responding to and identifying a familiar situation. Thus the toddler who begins to repeat the word *iddie* (kitty) when referring to the family pet is only adding one more way of knowing this familiar creature. The child has watched it, played with it, and knows that it meows, runs around, eats, and sleeps.

In this sense children's early language is based upon prior cognition; they already have many meanings. They know what orange juice looks like and how it tastes. They know that the cat scratches and jumps on the table. They have only to learn the words *juice* and *kitty* to apply the concepts they already have. (Pease & Gleason, 1985, p. 106)

During the second year, parent and child find many ways to collaborate in naming games. A favorite version is naming body parts, especially those on the face. Another version is reading picture books in which the child is asked to repeat the names of pictured items. Indeed, all familiar situations begin to provide opportunities for discovering and repeating the names of things.

Wells (1986) points out that the quality of these collaborative efforts is shaped by caregivers in several key ways. First, "sheer quantity" of conversation is important to making progress in the task of talking. In essence, while all children learn to speak, those who have more conversational exchanges tend to progress more quickly in mastering conversation conventions.

Wells also indicates that one-on-one situations (one adult and one child) appear to be the most beneficial context for learning. At these times, it is helpful if the adults talk about things that interest the child—usually items in the immediate environment that have caught the child's attention—or about activities that the two of them participate in—dressing, bathing, playing, and so forth.

Also, as leaders in the exchange, adults need to use locutions especially suited to the child's level of maturity and experience.

> keeping their utterances short and grammatically simple, using exaggerated intonation to hold the child's attention and to emphasize the key words, limiting the topics talked about to what is familiar to the child, and frequently repeating and paraphrasing what they say. (Wells, 1986, p. 45)

As listeners, adults are called upon to go more than 50 percent of the distance to interpret children's meanings from their highly condensed speech. Given the one-year-old's limited language production of one or two words, the parent must use the context of the situation to aid interpretation. When the youngster says, "nana" (banana), for example, the parent needs to take into account whether it is a request (is the child hungry?), a statement of fact (bananas are visible in a nearby dish), or a reaction derived from the fact that bananas are such a favorite that the infant will eat them any time.

What is crucial to the entire process is that the adult and child, through mutually attending to one another and the action or object at hand, share, for a few moments, a common perspective. The adult must attempt to see the world through the eyes of the youngsters. In fact, Wells (1986) writes that in order for conversations to proceed "the adult needs to try to adopt the child's perspective and, in his or her next contribution to the conversation, to incorporate some aspect of what the child has just said [or done] and to extend it or invite the child to do so him- or herself" (p. 47). In other words, adults need to respond to the beginning talker by talking about the things she or he introduces and by elaborating or helping the child to elaborate the topic under discussion. A fine example of this kind of exchange is reproduced below. Eighteen-month-old Mark is looking out of the window at the birds in the garden (pp. 47–48).

MARK: Jubs [Birds].
MOTHER: (inviting Mark to extend his own meaning) What are they doing?
MARK: Jubs bread [Birds eating bread (?)].
MOTHER: (extending Mark's meaning) Oh, look! They're eating the berries, aren't they?
MARK: Yeh.
MOTHER: (extending and paraphrasing) That's their food. They have berries for dinner.
MARK: Oh.

Mark introduces the topic, answers his mother's request for more information, and listens to his mother's extended descriptions of the topic. Such exchanges are, of course, typical of the infant-turned-toddler and the caregiver. They represent milestones in the child's speech development, which began with wordless exchanges and, in the short time of a year-and-a-half, progressed to a relatively sophisticated verbal give and take.

TRUSTING THE LEARNING

All of us who have been parents and have watched in awe and excitement the developments of our infant's first year are still unprepared for the thrill we experience with the coming of the first words. At some point after the baby reaches ten months, one sound or another separates itself from the rest of the infant's vocalizing and begins to be used consistently to *name* someone or something—a parent, a sibling, a pet, a favorite toy, or some other equally familiar and important item in the child's life. At first we test the baby to see if it is actually happening. We present the person or thing again and again, repeating the name of the designated item—"Daddy . . . this is daddy . . . say daddy." When the infant obliges—"Dada"—we know that a turning point has been reached.

Our impulse is to celebrate the occasion, to call the relatives—especially if it is our firstborn—and to tell everyone that the baby is talking. Even though infants possess a very limited grasp of the verbal system, we welcome them immediately into the community of talkers. Moreover, we make no attempts to correct or perfect early speech ("No, dear, it's 'Dad—dee' . . . repeat after me . . . ."). Such requests would be out of place. Not to accept and celebrate these early efforts is, for most parents, unthinkable.

In fact, even though pronunciation and phrasing are far from conventional, we are not concerned. We accept, as Lucy Calkins (1986) puts it, the infant's approximations without worrying about whether the child will be saying "Dada" at age ten. We understand that participating in a world of talkers is all that is needed for the youngster to master the phrasing and pronunciation of his or her native tongue. We trust that the processes that have brought the repeating of the first words will continue to shape the child's speech development. As parents and as a culture we possess enormous confidence that the first idiosyncratic epithets will eventually be transformed into conventional speech. In short, we trust completely the informal teaching processes that characterize learning to speak.

Finally, the significance of the collaborative model of learning to speak needs to be underscored. Differences of context between home and school notwithstanding, the teaching/learning exchanges among babies and their caregivers represent the teaching/learning model that must guide the design of early childhood language programs. It must be remembered that nearly all children master the unique challenges posed by the task of learning to speak. Indeed, they come to school at age three or four quite capable of conversing with adults and peers. And they accomplish this complex feat with informal teaching. The same is not true of learning to read, despite the enormous efforts made by our schools and the extensive use of formal teaching methods such as worksheets, skill-drills, and the like. Chapter 2 examines early literacy learning and suggests that, contrary to popular belief, learning to read is very similar to learning to speak.

2

Emergent Literacy
Reading

The first questions I ask graduate students are, "How would you define reading?" and "How do you think children learn to read?" Without too much hesitation, they record their responses. Though this is usually their first course in teaching reading, most students tend to have firmly held beliefs about this area of education.

In response to the first question, students answer that reading is the ability to recognize and comprehend written words. It is, they say, when the child is able to pick up a book, sit down, open it up to the first page with print, and begin to repeat, accurately, the words on the page; at that point we can say that the child is reading. There is absolutely no disagreement regarding this definition.

A similar consensus is not immediately reached in student responses to the question of how children learn to read. Some emphasize learning processes of association and repetition—see, recognize, and pronounce words and sentences repeatedly—while others feel that mastering phonic rules is the key to reading. Students define this process as learning how each letter sounds and then grouping letters together to form words and then sentences. When questioned further, those in the former group generally agree that phonics should also be included as part of the learning process. Since, they reason, the letters of the alphabet represent the sounds of words, it must be necessary to understand the combining rules for sounds and letters in order to learn to read.

To their credit, students are not as convinced of the correctness of their response to the question of *how* children learn to read as they are in defining what reading is. If the process were simply a matter of learning phonics rules—with a little sight vocabulary thrown in—then why doesn't everyone become a reader? They are keenly aware of the failure rate of the schools in teaching reading. In fact, most can remember reading sessions in their elementary years when they witnessed a classmate stumble through a paragraph, unable to recall familiar words or use the teacher's repeated suggestion to "sound it out." Equally significant, students recall the humiliation felt by the stuttering reader and their own sense of frustration at having to listen to a largely incomprehensible rendition of the story. Most of all, they remember a sense of relief that by some stroke of luck they were not one of those children who "didn't get it." As might be suspected, the students in my class who may have experienced difficulties in learning to read do not readily admit it. The stigma as well as the pain they experienced lasts a long time.

These commonly held beliefs regarding the "what" and "how" of reading have been accepted by most literate adults for decades, if not centuries. The myth that continues to hold sway in most communities is that first grade is the "magic" year in which youngsters are introduced to primers and taught to decode the print on the pages. Recent research has exploded this view by revealing that reading abilities involve much more than identifying words and that the learning process begins in the first year of life.

Interestingly, the model that has been identified as crucial to the development of reading abilities is the same as that discussed in the previous chapter. Learning to read, like learning to speak, evolves in stages. Early stages of reading, like early efforts to talk, resemble their mature forms in only very limited ways. Further, just as the infant begins the process of speaking in collaboration with caring adults, so the little one becomes a reader through regular exposure to literacy activities modeled by and shared with family members.

"Emergent literacy" describes processes that have been identified as significant to learning to read and that take place long before the child enters first grade. An important book of the same name, edited by William Teale and Elizabeth Sulzby (1986), traces literacy learning during the preschool years. It is largely through the findings of these researchers and their colleagues that the myths that previously dominated our thinking can now be replaced by more substantive views of reading and writing development.

BEGINNING WITH BOOKS

The first experiences with books begin for many children in the middle of the first year. One day when my son, Hans, was about six months old, my mother arrived with two books in hand. They were of the cloth and cardboard types, which was especially useful because they could be handled and mouthed by an infant without being immediately destroyed. Both books had pictures of toys and animals but no print. One book was constructed so that when a page was pressed a noise resulted that appeared to be coming from the pictured animal. I was somewhat dubious about the value of these books.

My mother, however, was totally convinced of the rightness of introducing her grandson to books even at this early age. Apparently she had done it for me and my brother, and she considered it a normal first step. I watched her "read" with Hans on her lap while she held the book in front of them. I thought the process was quaint, and probably because it was enjoyable and helped fill the time, I, too, began regular "reading" sessions with my six-month-old.

In the last decade, this kind of interaction with books between caregivers and infants has been recorded and analyzed in detail (Bruner, 1983; Snow & Ninio, 1986). These exchanges around books prove to be very instructive for infants. Similar to the collaborative efforts surrounding learning to speak and game playing, learning processes in picture-reading sessions are characterized by cooperation between caregiver and infant. In the following example, the child, Richard, is 13 months old. The "lap" method—child on mother's lap with book held in front of them—is used (Bruner, 1983, p. 78).

MOTHER: Look!
RICHARD: (Touches picture)
MOTHER: What are those?
RICHARD: (Vocalizes a babble string and smiles)
MOTHER: Yes, they are rabbits.
RICHARD: (Vocalizes, smiles, and looks up at mother)
MOTHER: (Laughs) Yes, rabbit.
RICHARD: (Vocalizes, smiles)
MOTHER: Yes. (Laughs).

In book-sharing episodes of the next several months, this same general sequence is followed by Richard and his mother. First, she directs Richard's attention to the picture, asks what is pictured, and gives the answers in response to his babbling. Bruner points out that the sequence is very similar to the game format, which, at this point in Richard's experience, is well established. In both activities, mother and Richard take turns, each playing a particular role with a predictable sequence. Similar to game playing, as picture-reading episodes are repeated, Richard becomes increasingly responsive, answering accurately his mother's requests and/or pointing to the pictured items himself and supplying the names.

In repeated encounters with picture reading, babies are introduced to key aspects of how books work. They are inducted into what Catherine Snow and Anat Ninio (1986) have aptly referred to as the "contracts of literacy" (pp. 121–38). It is in the activity of picture reading with an adult that the child begins to be "tutored in the special rules that hold for literate, but not for face-to-face, encounters" (p. 122). One of these contracts involves the symbolic nature of books. An important difference between game playing and book reading is that instead of the activity focusing on the manipulation of a toy, in book reading infant and caregiver are responding to a nonconcrete, pictured item. At first, many infants scratch the page, attempting to "lift" the pictured item out of its two-dimensional frame. They are told, of course, that this is a futile activity ("No, this is a picture of a cat, not a real cat."). Slowly the infant comes to understand the differences between the two-dimensional world of pictures and the real world of people and of things that can be squeezed, chewed, smelled. In these early book-sharing sessions, then, there is systematic emphasis on responding to representations of things, not the things themselves. The representation of things not present is of key significance in learning how to deal with the world of print. Eventually, symbols of things become the major mode for learning.

A further understanding about books is taught through the picture-reading procedure. Infants learn that an appropriate response to seeing a picture is to repeat the name of the item pictured. As Snow and Ninio (1986) point out, this is "highly artificial behavior . . . [since children's] habitual mode of interaction with objects is to act on them physically" (pp. 132–33). The act of repeating names of things has been long established as a part of the collaboration between child and caregiver in learning to talk. However, in oral versions of the labeling game, the name is given at the same time that the object is presented or an action is in progress. To ask that the infant transfer the naming response to something as abstract as an image of a thing—something the child has not actually seen "in the flesh"—is a big step. Eventually, of course, it is the print that becomes the focus of attention, and the "naming" of word-concepts that supplies the meaning of the text. Meanwhile, the fact that infants and toddlers become accomplished participators in the picture-labeling contract is further evidence of their remarkable abilities to symbolize experience.

Another contract to which the child must become a "signer" is the acceptance of the book as the "leader" of the activity (Snow & Ninio, 1986, p. 124). The sequence of the pictures in the book is the focus of the joint attention of child and caregiver. In the game format, as noted, the moves are controlled by the game script; in "peek-a-boo," appearing and disappearing of people and/or things determines the sequence of the activity. In contrast, looking at books has relatively little action, and the action that is involved goes on largely in the mind, where the "play" is with images. Again, through repeated experiences the child slowly discovers more to see and "read" in the pictures of favorite books.

Finally, in these early months the child is taught book-handling skills. The repeated message of the caregiver is that books are to be read, not mouthed or manipulated in inappropriate ways. In our language group, they are held "right side up" and pages are turned from left to right. As experiences with books mount, the infant-turned-toddler becomes more and more capable of turning the pages and anticipating the sequence of pictures of familiar books.

GITI: SHARING THE READING

If I was reluctant to begin picture-book reading when my son was an infant, when he became a toddler, I became an avid and eager storybook reader. Indeed, I began storytimes even before there was much tolerance on Hans' part for listening to an entire book at one sitting. Similar to game playing, in order for story reading to proceed at all, it had to be conducted as a joint activity. Some excellent samples of this kind of shared reading have been collected by Marcia Baghban (1984) from her reading to Giti, her two-year-old daughter. According to Baghban's descriptions, these story sessions could take place at any time during the day and were often initiated by Giti: "If I was sitting alone and Giti wanted me to read, she would select a book, stand in front of me and back up with book in hand" (p. 26). The following recording of Giti (right column) and her mother (left column) was made when Giti was 24 months old (pp. 141–42):*

Do you want to read this one by yourself?	No, no. (She pushes *Summer Friends* at me to read.)
Let's read it together. *Summer Friends.* This one is called *Summer Friends.* At the end of the summer, Susie said, "Tomorrow we are going back home to the city."	At end. Tomorrow we home city. (She echoes while mom
So Susie went to say goodbye to all her summer friends. Good.	reads.) [friyns]
She went to the meadow. "Goodbye Mr. Grasshopper," she said.	Grasshopper.
"Would you like to come to the city with me?"	Oh no.
"Oh no," said the grasshopper. "I couldn't jump in the city streets." She went to the Cow. "Goodbye, Mrs. Cow. Would you like to come to the city with me?"	Oh no.
"Oh no. You don't have such green grass in the city."	Oh no. You have green grass city. (Giti echoes mom.)

* Reprinted with permission of Marcia Baghban and the International Reading Association.

She went to the ducks.	
"Hello, little ducks. Would you like to come to	
the city with me?"	Oh no.
"Oh no," said the ducks, "We couldn't come to	
the city with you. We live in the pond."	
She went to the frog.	Frog. Bunny rabbit.
She went to the bunny rabbit.	She went to the frog.
She went to the birds.	The birds.
She went to the flowers.	
But no one, not even one, would go to the city	
with Susie. Susie felt very sad. She thought and	
thought and then she knew what she would do.	
What would she do? Let's turn the page.	
With her big box of crayons on a big	Paper.
white paper, she drew her summer friends.	
She drew the grasshopper.	
She drew the frog.	
She drew the ducks.	Susie drawing.
She drew the bunny.	
She drew the birds.	
That's Susie drawing.	Susie drawing.
Here's the picture that Susie drew. And there's	
everything. Susie's drawing. Is Susie happy?	Susie happy.
Good.	

Two-year-old Giti is an active and experienced participator in story sessions. Not only does she echo phrases her mother reads, she also anticipates the story sequence. Like many toddlers, she has favorite books, which she enjoys hearing over and over again. The repetition enables her to slowly absorb the story line, to anticipate repeated phrases, and to supply them at the appropriate moment in the text (for example, "Oh no."). As her mother reads the print, Giti "reads" the pictures and, at times, expands on the story through what she sees represented in the illustrations.

Another sample, recorded two months later, shows Giti and her mother sharing the reading of *Old MacDonald Had a Farm* (Baghban, 1984, p. 143).*

Can you read this book for me?	eieieiei. eieieiei.
Good.	eieieieieieie.
That's O.K.	eieieieieie.
What is this?	He had some chicks.
Yeah.	Chick chack here chick eieieieieiei.

*Reprinted with permission of Marcia Baghban and the International Reading Association.

What are these?	Ducks.
What do ducks do?	Kack, kack. eieieiei.
What are these?	Here? Hum.
Are they turkeys?	Turkeys. Yeah.
What do turkeys do?	Kack, kack, kack. Gooble, gooble, gobble.
eieieieiei.	
Good.	Oink, oink, oink, here.
Oink, oink.	Kack, here.
What are these?	Moooooo.
	They have bells.
Where are bells? Show me the	They have bells on their neck.
bells.	
Right. Oh wow.	Moooo. eieieieiei.

Mother and Giti finish the book with Giti supplying the choruses of animals sounds followed by the inevitable "eieieiei's" and the naming of items her mother points to in the pictures. At one point Giti says "hay," and her mother, following Giti's gaze, searches for the hay in the picture and comments, "Hay, right. Near the barn." At another point, the mother's request for a label for "apples" is responded to with an entire description: "They have apple on the tree." Through her mother's prompting and encouragement, Giti has become a rather accomplished picture-reader. The two of them follow one another's leads in focusing on different aspects of the illustrations.

This second sample is particularly revealing of the impact of patterned text—rhyme, rhythm, and repetition—on Giti's response to the book. Her mother's invitation to read the book prompts Giti to sail into multiple choruses of her version of "ee-i-ee-i-o." As the story in song proceeds, the familiar sequencing of animals, the noises they make, and the chorus help Giti to participate equally with her mother in the reading/singing of the book.

The third, and final, recorded sample shows Giti at two-and-a-half sharing the reading/labeling of a book (*Big Bird and Little Bird,* one of the Sesame Street series) with her mother (Baghban, 1984, pp. 145–46).*

Let's read one of your books. How about this one? You were going to read this one in the car this morning. Remember, *Big Bird and Little Bird.* You want to put it there? (Mom motions to table.) O.K. you just hold it flat on your lap.	
	Big Bird and Little Bird. (She reads the cover.)

* Reprinted with permission of Marcia Baghban and the International Reading Association.

Big Bird and Little Bird. (She reads
the title page.)
Big Bird and Little Bird. (She reads
the first page.)

Yeah.
What's this say?   I love balloons.
Good.   I love fountains.
Un huh.   I love whales.
Keep reading.   I love big boats.
What happens after that?   I love big mountains.
Ohhhh.   I like to feed the hippopotamus.
                                          See the balloon. (She points.)

Um hum.
Good. It's flying in the air.
Ohhh.   I like to feed the bunny.
                                          Who's that?
Isn't that Grover?   Grover.
                                          What's that?
I don't know. Another muppet.   It's a man.
A man. O.K.

                                          Oh, what's that?
                                          Oh, what's that, Mommy?
                                          (louder)
A baton.   A baton.
Um hum.
What's this one?   Accordion.
Good. Tuba.   Tuba.
Do you know this word?   [sese] you. (Sesame Street)
O.K. Let's turn the page. You read it.
You're almost finished.   You read it. I can't read it.
You read it all the time.
O.K. I'll finish it.

Giti begins this session by doing the reading. While we don't know if it is
the text that she is "reading," we do know that Giti is leading the session,
reconstructing the story line as she has come to understand it in previous
readings with adults. When she protests and asks that her mother continue,
her mother reminds her that she can do it. Sensing, apparently, that Giti has
done all the reading she's going to do, the mother finishes the book. As she
completes the story, Giti participates with the kinds of behaviors recorded in
earlier samples. She echoes names/labels or supplies them upon request and
anticipates the progress of the story by running ahead of the reading and
supplying key words of the text. In a relatively short period of time Giti has
expanded her range of reading behaviors from listener to initiator and leader

of story sessions. Wisely, her mother doesn't insist that Giti always perform the more mature roles. Such a demand would undermine the encouraging and cooperative tone that characterizes their story-sharing sessions.

Indeed, Marcia Baghban's sensitive and relaxed interactions with her toddler are related to the steady expansion of Giti's range of responses to books. Their storytimes are collaborative in nature. Giti indicated early on in their sessions together that she wanted to be a part of the process, and her mother doesn't miss an opportunity to let her contribute or take the lead. What Baghban extends to Giti is the chance to read by exploring the book in ways appropriate for a two-year-old. In the beginning, Giti, like Jonathan in the peek-a-boo game, played a more passive role. Slowly, however, she was able to assume—like Jonathan—the leadership role, which she had often watched her mother play. Though Giti accepts her mother's invitation to read *Big Bird and Little Bird,* the transcript reveals it is still a shared activity. The mother continues to prompt (What happens then? What does that say?), but Giti leads the page turning and decides where to focus in the text. What Baghban offers Giti, then, is the opportunity to hold the book, turn the pages, and sequence the storytelling in an encouraging, turn-taking situation with her.

Interestingly, all of the recordings of Giti and her mother begin with the suggestion that Giti read. Typically, adults do not pose this kind of invitation to toddlers. It is these invitations, in fact, that highlight new perspectives regarding what reading is and how it develops. What we are witnessing is the use of the term "reading" to define a far broader set of behaviors than were considered at the beginning of this chapter. Baghban's definition of reading is a set of responses that includes all of the many ways it is possible to share books. It need not, given the age/stage of a child, include behaviors specifically related to decoding strategies or word recognition. The fact that Giti is not producing an exact rendition of the text, a more mature reading behavior, is a mere formality. What Giti is doing is far more important. She is revealing her grasp of an important function of written language—to tell a story of people and things that are not present. In Snow and Ninio's (1986) terms, she has mastered one of the basic contracts of literacy; she understands that books represent "an autonomous fictional world" (p. 135). Snow and Ninio describe the significance of this understanding: "Full literacy skill involves the ability to create and comprehend realities that depend for their existence entirely on language" (p. 136). Through the regular engagement with books, Giti has become a participant in the fictional world created by language, a world that exists entirely in the imagination and, unlike other experiences in the toddler's life, does not possess a concrete existence. Again, what we are witnessing is the remarkable powers of abstraction and imagination that toddlers develop in collaboration with experienced participators in the world of fiction.

ROBYN: INDEPENDENT READING

In addition to shared storytimes with adults, Giti also explored books by herself. According to her mother, she liked to read to her dolls. A sample of this kind of independent book reading by a toddler, Robyn, age two-and-a-half, is recorded below. It is taken from Don Holdaway's book, *The Foundations of Literacy* (1979). Like Giti, Robyn comes from a "book-oriented" family. One of Robyn's favorite books is P. D. Eastman's *Are You My Mother?* (1960). It is about a baby bird who hatches when its mother is off looking for food. The plot revolves around the baby bird's search for its missing mother. The text, with identifying page numbers, is given in the left column, and Robyn's version, in the right column. Robyn begins the story at the point of hatching (Holdaway, 1979, pp. 43–44).

8 The egg jumped. It jumped and jumped! Out came the baby bird.

It jumped and jumped. Out the baby bird. (She then turns two pages impulsively as she is in the habit of doing.) He looked up and down. (Now another two pages.)

12 He looked up. He did not see her. He looked down. He did not see her.

16 Down, out of the tree he went. Down, down, down! It was a long way down.

Looked down, down, down, down. (Another two pages.)

20 He did not know what his mother looked like. He went right by her. He did not see her.

Go wound the big wock.

22 He came to a kitten. "Are you my mother?" He said to the kitten. The kitten just looked and looked. It did not say anything.

"Are you my mother?" "No," said the cat.

24 The kitten was not his mother, so he went on. Then he came to a hen. "Are you my mother?" he said to the hen. "No," said the hen.

Den e came a hen. "Are you my mudder?" "No," said the hen. . . .

[There is a gap in the transcript at this point, due to Robyn's confused rendition of syntactically complex material in the next 20 pages. We pick up her reading of the book at page 44.]

44 Just then, the baby bird saw a big thing. This must be his mother! "There she is!" he said. "There is my mother!"

Den e came a big thing. "Are you my brudder-mudder big thing?" . . .

46 He ran right up to it. "Mother, Mother! Here I am, Mother!" he said to the big thing.

"No," said mudder big thing.

48 But the big thing just said, "Snort." "Oh you are not my mother," said the baby bird. "You are a Snort. I have got to get out of here."

Itsa Snort!

50 But the baby bird could not get away. The Snort went up. It went way, way up. And up, up, up went the baby bird. [The Snort scoops up the baby bird and places him in his nest.]

Went up, up, up up "Werya going put may—baby bird?" In the back the tree.

When Mama bird returns to the nest she meets her baby and the story ends happily.

What Holdaway (1979) emphasizes is that while Robyn's rendering of the text is not exact or syntactically correct, the meaning, or "deep structure," of the story remains intact. He points out that what the recording reveals is how toddlers process story ideas: "They have encoded the *meanings* of the story into a unique structural form. They have remembered very little at the surface verbal level: what they have remembered most firmly is meanings" (p. 44). This is similar to the way in which children learn to speak. As noted, they don't imitate adult phrases verbatim; rather, they fasten onto names/labels of key people and things in their lives and repeat these enthusiastically at appropriate moments. The process is one in which children reconstruct the rules of speech, expanding syntax and vocabulary as they slowly move toward the conventional or mature model. Similarly, learning to read is largely a process of reconstructing meanings or story content. A vivid example of this process is children's reenactments of favorite books, which are largely faithful to the meanings in the original but have been transposed into children's unique language constructions.

CALL IT READING

Baghban and Holdaway are emphatic about how we should label the behaviors of our youngsters who incorporate these kinds of reading activities into their time spent with books: They are readers and should be acknowledged as such. Citing the growing literature documenting these activities, Baghban and Holdaway point out that Giti and Robyn are not exceptions. All children who engage in this kind of activity think of themselves as readers. Adults, these researchers suggest, must do the same. Our attitude has been to treat this kind of behavior as cute, even interesting, but not the real thing because it does not fit the circumscribed definition most of us hold regarding what constitutes "real" reading. As a result we use terms like "pretend reading" or "prereading" to describe this behavior.

This contrasts dramatically with the attitude adults bring to children's beginning attempts at speech. As noted when the infant begins to regularly attach an imprecise but recognizable label to a familiar object, we do not describe that as "prespeaking" or "pretend speaking." Rather, we are quick to assert that the baby is *talking,* and we understand that these early efforts will eventually develop into full-fledged speech (Baghban, 1984, p. 102). The fact, then, that speaking and reading develop in stages and that earlier forms have different characteristics from later stages should not deter us from considering our youngsters as speakers or readers when they are at the beginning of the process.

Finally, the most significant feature of reading for toddlers is the pleasure they derive from the activity (Baghban, 1984; Holdaway, 1979; Teale, 1984). At first, it is the sharing of the activity with favorite adults that accounts for their delight. As preschoolers add reading to themselves (or their friends or dolls) to their repertoire of responses to books, they reveal their growing abilities to recreate a story told in words on their own. These toddlers do not have to be cajoled into story sharing or reading. Rather, they are often the initiators of reading sessions and are highly precise about which books tell which stories and which book they want to read at a given time. "Almost all book experiences have been highly satisfying so that the children gradually develop unshakably positive expectations of print, and powerful motives to learn how to interpret for themselves" (Holdaway, 1979, p. 52). It is, then, largely the pleasure of sharing stories that makes readers of most of our young children.

3

Emergent Literacy
A World of Print

Though of key significance in literacy development, early book experiences represent only one category of exposure to written language for preschoolers. Studies of family life by William Teale (1986) and Denny Taylor (1983) reveal that there are many ways in which print is used in the home. Examples of common uses of print in the home and their significance to children's literacy learning are described below.

PRINT FUNCTIONS AND FAMILY LIFE

Foremost among the functions of print is taking care of daily routines. Grocery lists, calendars annotated with weekly events, the filling out of forms, paying bills, cooking, and traveling to work are some of many daily activities mediated by print. Not an end in itself, print facilitates these processes; it helps to "get things done" (Teale & Sulzby, 1986, p. xviii). Youngsters witness these uses of print as they accompany caregivers to the store or the bank and watch them use recipes or fill out forms for various organizations.

Another activity mediated by print is the social network that is supported by the writing of notes and letters to friends or relatives. Such activities have great appeal for toddlers when they are invited to share in the process. In Giti's case (Baghban, 1984), her grandparents lived far away from where she lived. As a result she received notes and cards from them through the mail. These notes prompted Giti to respond with her own notes. According to her mother, cards with drawing/writing were carefully stuffed in envelopes and "addressed" to Grandma or Grandpa. An outgrowth of sending and receiving notes was getting to know the postal services. An important routine for Giti was the daily trip to the lobby of the apartment building to get the mail. Her mother writes that the "junk" mail belonged to Giti.

One of her favorite play activities at 21 months was writing on print. She would attack the fourth class mail, newspapers, and flyers just to scribble on the writing. If one side of an advertisement was blank, she would turn it to the side with the writing and scribble all over it. (p. 50)

Another form of written communication, writes Taylor (1983), is the sending and receiving of notes among family members living under the same roof. Toddlers with school-age siblings may observe them write a note to Mom and Dad and put it in a prominent place so it won't be missed when the parents return from an evening out. Mothers also tuck notes in lunch boxes to be read by their grade-schoolers later in the day. These messages may contain reminders about after-school plans, or they may be just a way to keep in touch while physically separated.

Then, too, in today's world, most homes need print to organize entertainment schedules. Newspapers and TV guides are prominent in this category and represent some of the first items school-age youngsters attempt to master. Newspapers and magazines are also important to family members for gathering information about local, national, and international events. According to Teale (1986), keeping up-to-date about certain activities is important to people who make a habit of sharing their views with family, friends, or co-workers with similar interests. In addition to political happenings, many people enjoy following sports events or keeping up with the lives of celebrities.

Both Taylor (1983) and Teale (1986) point out that written material related to school activities are key forms of print that flow to and from homes with school-age children. In addition to daily homework, there are notes from teachers and administrators announcing special events, meetings, or fund raising activities. Interestingly, in many homes preschoolers may observe not only their siblings but also their parents engaged in homework. This is the case with three-year-old Chris, the son of Frank Fortney, one of my graduate students. Frank uses his computer to fulfill most writing assignments. According to Chris' father, this instrument fascinates Chris.

[Chris] expressed an interest in writing on the "puter" also. Several times now, before I begin [my work], he sits on my lap and asks me to show him the letters that spell the names of all the family members. I point to the key and he taps it. When we are done, he reads the names and then allows me to get to work. Chris has also begun to recognize the letters of his name in the environmental print around him. He points with glee to the letter *C* whenever he spies it. The letters *i* and *s* also catch his attention. (Fortney, n.d.)

Figure 3.1   *Chris's writing*

Through these kinds of experiences, Chris is exposed to the functions print can serve, and he is also learning something about print forms—namely, letter names and shapes. Chris' mother has organized special drawing/writing materials for him and has spent time showing him the shapes of the letters of his name. Frequently, his father says, Chris brings his writing equipment to the table where his older brothers do their homework and "works" along with them (see Figure 3.1). Note the presence of *C*'s and *i*'s in his productions. Such episodes form another category of print exposure for the toddler. This one, however, is qualitatively different from the others "because the focus of the activity [is] to help another person . . . learn to read and write" (Teale, 1986, p. 187). In these episodes, then, the major focus of the activity is the forms of written language rather than their functions. What needs to be emphasized is that these moments of "teaching" are fleeting and informal. No demands for a particular performance are made. Rather, caregivers model writing forms and allow toddlers to take the lead in giving feedback about what they are learning.

A significant part of these early encounters with print is the choice of words through which introductions to the alphabet are made. Almost without fail, parents choose the child's own name and later add names of family

Figure 3.2 *Giti's "G"*   (Source: Baghban, 1984, p. 67)

members. These are the names, of course, that hold the most interest and meaning for the toddler. As noted, when preschoolers begin to discover "their letters" in the print around them, they gleefully call out, "There's my name" or "There's me." Similar to Chris' experience, the first recognizable letter form in Giti's writing was the first letter of her first name. According to her mother (Baghban, 1984), she would write *G*'s "from the bottom to the top, point to what she had done, and say /diydiy/ for her own name, Giti. Enraptured by the representation, she practiced *G* in isolation . . . on masses of paper" (p. 55). Figure 3.2 (Baghban, 1984; used with permission) is the first spelling of Giti's entire name, produced when she was two-and-a-half. The outline of the *G* is clear; the (ˆ) is her "version of the joint at the finish of the *G*" (p. 67); and the remaining marks are the i–t–i with two dots. Around the same time, Giti began to recognize the logos of familiar chain stores. McDonalds ("onalds") was a favorite, and peaks representing the *M* began to appear in her productions.

Infants and toddlers, then, are surrounded by a world of print. As a result, writes Teale (1986), "virtually all children in a literate society like ours have numerous experiences with written language before they ever get to school" (p. 192). As noted, the emphasis in these exposures is on the functions of language—its capacity to get things done—rather than its forms. It has only been in the last decade that the significance of the toddler's experience with literacy functions as part of the literacy learning process has been recognized.

DIFFERENCES IN FAMILY LITERACY PATTERNS

Families differ significantly in the quantity and quality of their uses of print. Teale (1986) writes that some children have opportunities "to observe much more reading and writing going on around them" than others do; some have much more experience "interacting with parents or older siblings in activities which involve literacy"; and, finally, many youngsters spend more time in independent "reading" and "writing" activities than others do (p. 192). What these differences add up to is that some youngsters enter school programs with far more experience with literacy functions and forms than other youngsters have.

There is major contrast in the amount and kind of literacy activities related to different jobs, as reflected in Teale's study of lower-middle-class households and Taylor's data from middle-class homes. In the professions, specific parts of the work require reading and writing. And as the popularity of briefcases attest, frequently some of this work is performed at home. This is not true of most industrial and service jobs. Income level is related to type of job. Teale makes the point that more money to spend means more ways to spend money and, as a result, more uses of print needed to support the spending (such as travel brochures, advertisements for consumer goods, and directions for use of consumer products).

Economics, however, tends to play a less crucial role in exposing youngsters to a variety of print functions than do the attitudes toward written language modeled by important people in their lives. Different cultural practices among family groups significantly influence home uses of print. The use of magazines and newspapers as well as the reading of books differ significantly across households. For some, these print materials are used daily for entertainment and information gathering, while for others TV and radio are the main resources serving such goals. It is largely the habits of family and friends that influence the degree of people's reliance on print to fulfill needs in these categories. The effect on the preschooler of family differences in kind and quantity of uses of print is deep and long lasting. If parents always find time at the beginning or end of the day to read the newspaper or a book, their children are likely to adopt such habits as they grow up. Likewise, in homes in which reading of books for pleasure, information, or education is not part of the daily activities, observant youngsters have little or no reason to suppose that such experiences are pleasurable and/or useful.

Participation in the storytime category is also related to differences in cultural practices across households. While regular adult/child story-sharing sessions are a staple of many homes, other families, writes Teale (1986), do not engage in such activities. When these youngsters reach school age, they tend to be less competent in handling books and understanding how print works than, say, Giti and Robyn, who were experienced book sharers and readers by the time they were four years old. As noted, approaching the world of books requires repeated experiences in which caregivers collaborate with children in building an understanding of book conventions as well as story structure.

Recent research confirms that the child's early experiences in sharing storytimes are significant to their future literacy development (Heath, 1983;

Teale, 1984, 1986; Wells, 1986). Because the variation in children's pre-school literacy experiences is so great, the schools must respond accordingly. The challenge for early childhood educators is to provide appropriate experiences for youngsters who come to school very knowledgeable about books and literacy functions as well as for those who lack such understanding.

IMPLICATIONS FOR EARLY EDUCATION

Commonly held beliefs about what reading is and how it is learned were described at the beginning of Chapter 2. In light of the past decade of research in literacy development, those beliefs are now understood to be wholly inadequate. Indeed, to define the entire process of engagement with print as simply the recognition of the words or the learning of "the sounds letters make" is as dangerous as it is erroneous. Not only do such beliefs motivate the design of misguided teaching methods, but they also obscure an appreciation of the significance of children's early reading behaviors that have nothing to do with learning the alphabet or word identification.

Based on the research evidence of the past decade, we are now in a position to articulate criteria for designing programs in early literacy. First, this means placing storytimes and an examination of children's literature at the center of the curriculum. Further, methods of investigating these materials must be modeled after the informal, shared-reading episodes typical of storytimes in the home. As we will see, the challenge of fulfilling the needs of both those who come to school with many literacy experiences as well as those who come with very few can be met more successfully by adopting collaborative methods than by using the formal teaching methods found in most early childhood classrooms.

In recent years, the difficulties of dealing with children who come to school lacking consistent and pleasurable experiences with books and other print materials have been compounded by pressures to implement formal teaching methods—use of workbooks and skill-drill activities—at earlier and earlier ages. I have heard nursery and kindergarten teachers insist that they don't have time to read books to their groups because of all the other materials they must cover to prepare their students for reading programs in the coming years! Previously, this kind of Catch-22 situation with regard to early reading programs could have been tolerated because of a lack of understanding of the significance of experiences with books in relation to learning to read. This is no longer the case, and the fact that many beginning literacy programs do not engage youngsters in careful and consistent experiences with books is no longer acceptable. The saddest outcome of such programs is that the youngsters who most need a strong literature program—those with little or no grasp of book language or story sense—remain at a critical disadvantage in their reading development. An understanding of story structures only comes with many experiences of listening to and sharing books. Developing such an understanding must be the highest priority for children who haven't had such experiences by the time they get to the nursery or kindergarten classroom.

Equally significant in designing early literacy programs is revising our notions regarding the teaching of the forms and functions of written language. Previously it was thought that the major method for teaching beginning reading and writing should be an intensive exploration of letter/word forms. Thus children have been required to sit at tables, hold pencils, and follow dots outlining the letters of the alphabet or short words. Such a program is in total contrast with infants' and toddlers' home learning environments, in which they are introduced to the functions of print *first* through their participation in family living. In these settings, learning letter names or shapes tends to be embedded in functional tasks. Schools reverse this approach and place greater emphasis on the teaching of forms than on the teaching of functions of language. Equally problematic, in school programs youngsters are taught print forms almost entirely divorced from meaningful contexts or functions. Again, such counterproductive procedures tend to be more injurious to those who begin school with less knowledge about print functions than those who have observed a great many uses of print in their homes. As we shall see, the classroom setting lends itself nicely to continuing and enhancing the development of children's awareness of how print gets things done, at the same time that it provides opportunities to explore print forms.

Finally, a major criterion for the design of early literacy programs is the development of instructional strategies in which collaboration guides teaching/learning experiences. Gordon Wells (1986) has identified key characteristics of this approach. It is based on two assumptions about learners and teachers. The first is that learning "involves an *active reconstruction* of the knowledge or skill that is presented, on the basis of the learner's existing internal model of the world" (p. 118). In short, the traditional emphasis on learning as imitating-the-teacher (teaching-as-telling) must be replaced by many opportunities for initiation by students. It "calls for the *negotiation* of meaning, not its unidirectional transmission" (p. 118). The second assumption underlying collaborative education is that the teacher must listen to what students have to say and to try to see the world from their perspectives. "Only then," writes Wells, "can the teacher's contribution have that quality of [personal and meaningful] responsiveness that we have seen from the preschool years to be essential in helping the child develop his or her understanding" (p. 118).

Indeed, what has been described as the handover principle—the major strategy through which caregivers instruct their young in learning to talk, to play games, to read, and so forth—must be viewed as the major method for shaping classroom instruction. Such an approach is not entirely foreign to the traditional early childhood program in which teachers see their role as supporting the children's initiatives and helping them realize their goals in, say, block building or dramatic play. Too often, however, the approach does not extend beyond these areas of the program. It is especially lacking when teachers turn to the areas of the curriculum that involve symbols, that is, the famous three R's. Subsequent chapters describe how to design literacy programs based on collaborative teaching and learning experiences for early childhood classrooms from the nursery through the primary years.

Part II

THE THREE–YEAR–OLD

4

Classroom Life
The Social Context
of Language Learning

I stepped into Betsy Elliot's classroom to borrow some cooking equipment. As I collected the utensils, I became fascinated by the air of excitement that seemed to fill the room. Twelve three-year-olds were happily and noisily engaged in all areas of the room. I lingered for a few minutes to watch. Betsy was reading a story to a small group in the book corner, while her assistant was helping children at the puzzle table.

Suddenly, there was an outburst of high-pitched, angry voices. Two boys were struggling over one police officer's cap in the house corner. Betsy stood up, quietly made excuses to her group, and walked over to the boys. When she arrived, she leaned over and said something I couldn't hear. Both boys began talking excitedly while still holding onto the hat. Then, one leaned over and looked as if he was about to bite the other's hand. Betsy restrained him and without too much difficulty got one and then the other to relinquish his hold on the cap. I heard her invite each child to tell her what happened. Somehow a solution was hit upon—one would use the hat and the other would use a pair of white gloves, which Betsy dug out of one of the dress-up boxes, to direct traffic. I marveled at Betsy's calm and her patience. Though the disturbance had been of short duration, it had been very loud and, to me, very disruptive. At no point did Betsy raise her voice. The other youngsters, I noticed, glanced in the direction of the outburst but were not concerned. Clearly they were confident that one of the adults would take care of things. After what I witnessed, I could understand their confidence.

FROM HOME TO SCHOOL

As children move beyond the world of home and family, one of the first places they must become accustomed to is the classroom. The social actions

35

needed to negotiate life in a community of peers and adults pose a major challenge for the nursery-age child. The social community—so significant in the child's early learning in the home—is equally important as a medium for learning in the classroom. As noted, the success of the family as an educational force is largely derived from the collaborative nature of the social bonds between children and caregivers. Because of the crucial impact of the social environment on learning processes, including language and literacy learning, the most important and most difficult task for teachers of any grade level is shaping a collaborative class community.

The nature of the interactions between child and caregiver, described earlier as the key to language learning, provides guidelines for shaping life in the classroom.

Turn-taking: Teachers must model ways of sharing that children can slowly adopt for themselves.

Routines: Teachers must set up predictable patterns of living so that children are able to become increasingly independent in negotiating classroom life.

Sociability: Teachers need to help children understand and negotiate the complexities of interacting with peers. Teachers also need to understand that expressions of unfriendly behaviors are an inevitable part of developing mature social relations.

Language figures prominently in the young child's attempts to come to grips with life in the classroom. Children's initial attempts to get what they need or want through physical actions—grabbing and striking out—must be curtailed. "Use words" is the daily refrain of the teacher of young children. And as children adopt this method for threading their way through the school day, they slowly adopt increasingly mature methods for managing program demands and interacting with their peers.

Teachers must consciously model ways of interacting with children based on the handover principle; they must be aware that their actions toward youngsters provide the most vivid lessons of how to behave. The impulse on the part of teachers to force the adoption of acceptable behavior ("You must take turns!") undermines the entire collaborative approach. In such exchanges, the adult's actions and attitude give an opposite and much more powerful message than the words. Rather than negotiation, such behavior teaches children to use force or coercion in dealing with their class community. Unfortunately, children usually learn the lesson very well.

A few weeks after my visit to Betsy's room, I learned that she intended to take a year's leave of absence. I was invited to fill in for her as the teacher of the morning class of three-year-olds. Though I had had many years of experience working with five- through seven-year-olds, I had never taught three's. How long, I wondered, would it take me to understand life from a three-year-old perspective? Of no less importance, how long would it take me to respond with the kind of equanimity Betsy possessed when faced with the three-year-old's passionate and primitive expressions of feeling? Throughout that year, I kept a journal of what were to me the outstanding events of each week. What follows are excerpts from that journal which describe some of the doubts and difficulties I faced during what turned out to be an incredible year of learning through teaching.

Turn-taking

> *Episode:* This morning Kimberly was in the doll corner playing with Jessica. All was going very smoothly until there was a sudden outburst of screaming and crying from Kimberly and Jessica. I moved toward the doll corner and found the two of them hanging onto the same doll. Kimberly was shouting at the top of her lungs—"But we have to share!" By the time I had calmed the two of them, the issue of the doll had been forgotten.

I deduced that in Kimberly's previous school experience "turn-taking" was something that had been arbitrarily forced upon youngsters who were unable to comprehend its meaning. Though Kimberly had learned to repeat the phrase, "we have to share," it had no meaning for her. Indeed, its meaning was totally reversed. Her outburst indicated that sharing something, with all of the necessary negotiating of who will have what and when, was quite beyond her comprehension. As noted, with more forced moments of "sharing," Kimberly could come to understand classroom turn-taking as something that involves coercive rather than democratic actions.

Turn-taking, once a simple give and take between the child and an understanding caregiver, must now be mediated among a dozen or more classmates. Teaching children how this might be accomplished was one of my main tasks. If youngsters have been treated arbitrarily by adults either at home or in school, they are quick to adopt such a model. They will treat others as they have been treated, taking toys or materials at will without any sense of the give and take that must characterize sharing with another. All too often, youngsters having difficulty with sharing are further admonished with, "How would you feel if someone didn't want to share with you?" Such an admonition confuses as well as distorts the issue. What the adult is saying, in effect, is that even though no one is extending compassion toward the child, he or she is expected to show it to others. Such emotional empathy, which has its beginnings in these years, does not become a reliable response for most children until they move into the early and middle grades. Certainly, it will never be understood if caregivers and teachers insist that children adopt this response as if it were just a matter of changing one's attitude the way one changes shoes. Rather, adults must be the first to extend a genuine and consistently compassionate attitude toward youngsters. They must model ways and means for negotiating turn-taking so that eventually youngsters can assume responsibility for themselves in situations that require sharing. Finally, adults must understand that it takes many attempts and much tme to absorb and practice turn-taking in the classroom before these skills become a reliable part of the child's social behavior.

Routines

Episode: "Evelyn," I said as she approached the easel to paint, "you need to put on your apron. It's hanging on your hook in the bathroom." "No!" she said with finality. I tried to reason: "Evelyn, wearing an apron will keep paint from getting on your clothes." "No!" she repeated. I didn't want to bring on a confrontation; I had enough of these with Evelyn about things that were not negotiable, such as remaining in the room instead of visiting the secretaries in the office, or wearing her jacket at outdoor time. Her parents were in the process of separating, and she was understandably shaken by this event. "O.K., Evelyn," I responded, then added, as an afterthought, "not today but tomorrow." Evelyn said nothing and went off to paint.

Though it took many months for most of these three's to become acclimated to the schedule and the accompanying routines, none were as vocal in their resistance to adopting classroom patterns of living as Evelyn. The apron issue was not the only area of difficulty, but it was the most consistent. As the days and weeks went by, I continued to let Evelyn refuse to wear the apron. Each morning she never failed to request to paint, and I never failed to suggest the apron. When she refused, I always said that maybe tomorrow would be the day.

Six weeks later: Today, as usual, Evelyn came and asked to paint. Expecting a repetition of what had become our verbal ritual, I reminded her that she needed to put on her apron and I waited for her refusal. Instead, she began walking toward the easel, calling over her shoulder, "Tomorrow."

Certainly Evelyn's response revealed that she had come a long way—even if it was the wrong way. From my point of view, this was an example of the handover principle gone astray. While Evelyn had picked up my words, she indicated that she had not adopted my view of the situation. For her, our exchange had actually become a rather neat way to avoid, rather than comply with, the routine. I consoled myself with the thought that there had been so many difficult moments with Evelyn during the fall, it was probably just as well that she had taken charge of this exchange. The use of the apron per se was no longer the issue. What was at stake was my credibility—did I mean what I said, or didn't I?

Three weeks later, some finger paint arrived. I had set up a special table for this activity, which, for most three-year-olds, is very exciting. Everyone wanted a turn. When Evelyn came to ask for her turn, I said she needed to put on her apron. I realized the moment I said it that I was prepared to deny her a turn if she refused. As though sensing the change in my attitude, however, she went and got her apron without a word and brought it to me to help her put it on. We didn't talk about the fact that "tomorrow" had become "today"; indeed, the two of us just got to work putting on the apron as if this was something we did everyday—which it was from then on.

While the apron episode was, for me, the most memorable, there were other areas in which Evelyn and I debated the pros and cons of the demands of classroom life. In fact, during the year, most youngsters raised questions about one routine or another. Many youngsters who resisted routines felt, as Evelyn did, a sense of impotence because of changes taking place in their lives over which they had no control. Other youngsters exhibited this kind of resistance precisely because they had never been given consistent opportunities to make appropriate choices about their activities. And, I discovered, even youngsters who were quite happy about following routines and schedules at some points wanted opportunities to make decisions about their school life.

I began to realize that the points of conflict provide some of the best moments in which to explore and practice negotiation in classroom communities. Without these differences of opinion or this sense of need, teachers and students would not have opportunities to negotiate solutions. Through conflict, children learn to think things through and to make thoughtful decisions about their lives. Young people who become disenchanted with school as early as the elementary years do so in part because they feel as if they have so little input into shaping their time in school. The message for teachers is that we need to find ways and means in which youngsters are given opportunities to make choices in the design of classroom life.

Friendship

Episode: One morning in February, Becca walked up to Kimberly and asked, "Will you be my friend?" Kimberly didn't seem to know what to make of this question, but she nodded consent and waited to see what would happen next. Becca said something about playing in the house corner, which was what they did. Later in the morning, I heard Becca repeat to Kimberly and Jessica, who had joined them, "Let's be friends." Becca's statement, repeated in a confidential tone, prompted the girls to momentarily stop their play and look at her. Her eager, expectant expression apparently influenced both to nod their agreement.

Of all the relationships children explore in the classroom setting, making friends is arguably the most important to them. From the beginning of this process in the nursery years and continuing through adolescence, young people are most concerned about their relationships with their peers. When things go well, life is bright. When friendship is denied for whatever reasons, the "outcast" feels the deprivation keenly.

As the weeks went by, Becca continued to use the phrases "Will you be my friend?" and "Let's be friends." Soon many of the other girls were repeating these locutions to one another. Often the opener "Will you be my friend?" was asked and assent was given. Then the two "friends" were at a loss as to what to do. While these little girls were aware that the phrases identified an important part of life, they were not at all clear about what it was.

Three weeks later: This morning Becca and Kimberly were playing in the house corner. Both were a little cranky, but they had verbally vouched their friendship, and so far they had managed to sustain a restaurant game. However, at some point the play disintegrated, and Kimberly began shouting, "No, I won't be your friend!!" I arrived in time to restrain a very distraught and uncomprehending Becca from coercing "friendship" out of Kimberly by biting her. I guessed that Becca pestered Kimberly about the friendship issue, and Kimberly became frustrated at having to stop playing to debate or reconfirm this idea. "But she said she would be my friend!" Becca wailed over and over as she cried on my shoulder. Becca was having great difficulty accepting what she interpreted as Kimberly's change of heart. I tried to console Becca by telling her that just because Kimberly didn't want to play with her at the moment, didn't mean that they weren't friends. Becca was inconsolable.

The preoccupation with the idea of friendship has reached a peak. The phrase "I won't be your friend," which had by this time become as popular as "Will you be my friend?" had little real feeling behind it. Yet it often caused interruptions and breakdowns of communication between pairs of children.

At first, I found the primitive fashion in which these three's asked for and rejected friendship shocking. When the latter episodes occurred, I tended to place myself immediately in the shoes of the rejected youngster and to imbue the rejector with antisocial motives. As I continued to observe the transitory nature of their friendships, I realized that the youngsters used these phrases *in order to find out what they mean.* This realization cast the issue in a different light. I slowly came to understand that, similar to the resistance to routines, moments of conflict provided opportunities for the children to explore and experience the skills of seeking and maintaining friendships.

Name-Calling

Episode: It was a Friday morning in the middle of January and too cold to go outdoors. Short tempers and general crankiness would describe the tone of the group. Four youngsters were playing together at the sand table. I was near by straightening the dress-up corner and was only dimly aware that the group at the sand table was chanting something. I tuned in when Dan called to me:

DAN: Linda, they're calling me stupid.

KIMBERLY: You're a stupid . . . (repeats the phrase joyfully to Dan).

ME: (I look at Dan just as his expression starts to cave in. Moving closer to the group, I sit in a chair near them—just in time to catch Dan, who stumbles toward me, buries his face in my shoulder, and starts to cry.)

KIMBERLY: (Moves over to us immediately) Why is Dan crying?

ME: (I look closely at Kimberly to make sure her question is sincere, which it is. I turn to Dan.) Can you tell Kimberly why you're crying?

DAN: (No response)

ME: (Filling in) I think Dan's feelings are hurt because you were calling him "stupid." (I pause and then add) Did you mean to hurt his feelings?

KIMBERLY: (Shakes her head and is very solemn)

ME: Why don't you tell him that. It might make him feel better. (Kimberly watches Dan intently. She doesn't say anything so I begin to speak for her.) Dan, they didn't—

KIMBERLY: (Shakes her head at me and tries to put her hand over my mouth) Don't say it!

ME: (I stop. Kimberly moves around to the other side of Dan, who, though still in the circle of my arm, is watching her intently.)

KIMBERLY: Are you all finished crying now, Dan? (Since he doesn't say anything she turns to me.) Is he all finished?

ME: (To Dan) Are you all finished?

DAN: (Nods, still watching Kimberly)

KIMBERLY: I'm sorry Dan. I didn't mean to hurt your feelings. (Dan keeps looking at Kimberly without saying anything.) I'm sorry, Dan. I didn't mean to hurt your feelings. (Dan still doesn't say anything.)

ME: (Brightly) And now it's all over. Why don't you two go back to the sand table.

DAN: (moves out of my arm toward Kimberly and the sand table and takes my hand.) You come, too.

(I join them for awhile.)

In the world of the three-year-old, name-calling as a social activity is just getting started. The incident just described demonstrates that, like the testing of the dimensions of friendship through the use of certain phrases, it tends to have more of an investigative quality than a deliberately antisocial thrust. For adults witnessing a situation like this, however, it is very easy to assign motives. To my "experienced" adult eye, Kimberly was the aggressor and Dan was the victim. That I didn't act on that assumption was nothing short of a miracle.

The first hint that my usual assumptions needed to be put aside was when Kimberly asked, in utter sincerity, why Dan was crying. Her question was truly a revelation. After I repeated the question to Dan and he didn't respond, I moved in with my description of meanings and intents commonly assigned to this phrase. Kimberly appeared to have no difficulty understanding this explanation and also indicated that she did not intend to hurt Dan's feelings. I followed this with a suggestion about how Kimberly could clear up the misunderstanding by telling Dan she hadn't meant any harm. At this point, I was still struggling with my adult tendency to take charge of the episode and began to speak for Kimberly—just in case she couldn't or wouldn't act on my suggestion. Again, Kimberly acted in a most appropriate way. She gently hushed me so that she could say the words herself.

Adult reactions to antisocial phrases alert children to when and how they are used. This episode provided me with an opportunity to explain usual uses and motives for this kind of phrase. Eventually, youngsters begin to use name-calling as an expression of hostility. Like the infants who learn about the ways of the world from caregivers who interpret their actions for them, so nursery-age children learn what constitutes antisocial behavior from our reactions to and descriptions of their exploratory behaviors. We need, however, to exercise extreme caution in moving in with the assumption of "naughty" or hostile intents. The vulnerable little ones will tend to accept our interpretations of their actions regardless of their original intentions.

I could have put an end to the episode by saying something like, "We don't use those words here." At times, discussions are not possible, and the adult needs to terminate the children's actions. If, however, that approach becomes the main method for solving problems, then key opportunities for developing social skills are short circuited. Social conflicts, I realized once again, provide needed opportunities for children to practice skills in negotiating and taking responsibility for themselves. For teachers they provide moments in which to describe and define the nature of our social system. As a result, these episodes should be welcomed rather than avoided.

Then, too, Kimberly revealed how much she had grown. This was the same youngster who had, a few months ago, been totally confused about turn-taking. In this episode, she demonstrated just how thoughtful and sensitive she could be, given the chance to work through a conflict.

> *Five months later:* It was the last week of school. Just before going outdoors we always gathered at one large table for juice. I wasn't paying close attention to the juice table conversations until I heard Evelyn say to Dan, for no apparent reason, "You stupid!" Dan lowered his head and glowered at her. Then he said, "Linda, tell Evelyn there are no stupids in this room!" Completely taken in by Dan's assertiveness, I repeated the phrase as I had been directed.

Though the episode was brief, it was long in terms of Dan's growing up and becoming a full-fledged member of his peer group. To some extent he had been too easily hurt by the playful, fleeting thrusts and counterthrusts that are a part of three-year-olds' exchanges. He needed to develop some resilience and ability to defend himself should he be unfairly assailed. His mother and I had spoken about it. Dan was her only child, and the two of them were very good companions. She confided that she was aware of his acute sensitivity and that she was working with him to help him speak up for himself. Dan's angry but very mature phrase, "There are no stupids in this room," came out of his mother's discussions with him. When I shared the episode with her, she recognized the phrasing that she and Dan had practiced together.

CLASSROOM COLLABORATION

The difficulty of working with young children who don't hold mature views of, say, turn-taking or the skills of friendship is not to be underestimated. Nor can it be overlooked. Indeed, the chance to examine life from the child's perspective is what must intrigue as well as motivate an adult to take on the responsibility of teaching young children.

Further, those of us who want to teach must understand that the educational process is influenced as much by the nature of the social world of the classroom—the "how" of teaching—as it is by the content or program—the "what" of teaching. We have tended to emphasize the "what" and given much less consideration to the "how." The evolution of my understanding of classroom life from the three-year-old perspective shaped and reshaped how I interacted with these youngsters. The specific actions I took are not necessarily generalizable to other teachers and classrooms of children. Each episode is connected to a particular set of people and circumstances and, therefore, a particular set of solutions. The importance of my efforts lies in my desire to learn from children, the other, and often neglected, side of the coin of the desire to teach children.

The social climate in which young children learn definitively influences what they learn. Literacy learning, as noted, evolves through adult/child sharing of print functions and materials. The exchanges tend to be filled with pleasure and caring as the caregiver supports the child's fledgling efforts to grasp language uses and forms. In a socially unsupportive atmosphere, the child soon learns to dislike, or simply tune out, what the adult is attempting to demonstrate or teach. This is as true in the classroom as the home. Either teachers find ways to build collaborative social communities in their classrooms or their efforts to teach academic subjects, including reading and writing, will be largely wasted.

Because we who are teachers are so visible and so important to youngsters, they learn most conspicuously from us. They learn from all the actions we perform, not just those we have designated in our own minds as "teaching" moments. Children who are required to assume mature methods for sharing in the classroom—who, like Kimberly, must share or else—learn the opposite of what is taught. They learn that social relations in the classroom are coercive and dictatorial rather than charitable and democratic. Children learn how to share gracefully in a group situation from teachers who model such behavior by tolerating the time it takes for youngsters to understand, to reinvent for themselves, ways of giving and taking with their peers. Children learn to become responsible for themselves and their actions when they are given opportunities to speak for themselves, to present their views, and to have their ideas considered. This kind of active search for ways to evaluate and resolve problems is precisely what is required of students as they progress further and further in their lives in and out of school. We cannot complain that elementary or high school students are lacking active and independent responses to their education, if we have not made sure that their first and most impressionable school experiences have provided opportunities for them to shape their school life.

Finally, the social issues discussed in this chapter are not idiosyncratic to nursery classrooms; rather, they represent concerns relevant to all early childhood, elementary, and high school classrooms in our society. Teachers who claim that they have "no problem" with social relations or no classroom conflicts with their particular age group have simply created a classroom social system in which they have eliminated the possibilities for collaboration. What they have created instead is an entirely teacher-directed social system in which adult prescriptions for living must be subscribed to by students. Classrooms that do not provide, as a part of their educational agenda, regular opportunities for discussing and exploring, for example, allocation of class space and time, dimensions of friendship, and antisocial behaviors overlook the most significant area of teaching and learning that classroom life can provide—the possibility of children contributing to the shaping of their classroom community, the social world beyond their family life, and the replica of their future life as citizens and contributors to society.

5

The Sense of Story
Building Classroom Culture

At the start of my second day teaching three-year-olds, I saw Becca pick up a puzzle and hold it on her lap. I sat down beside her, ready to help in any way that might seem appropriate. As it turned out all I needed to do was listen. The puzzle was a typical one for that age—circles in red, triangles in yellow, and squares in blue. Each shape was represented in four graduated sizes. Becca picked up the smallest triangle, looked at me, and said, with much delight, "A tiny!" Then she picked up the next triangle and, after a slight pause, said, "A small." The next piece in line was picked up. Becca looked at it with eyes wide in mock surprise and named it, "A big." With the final piece, Becca held it in her hand for a moment and said in a tone of playful respect, "A giant!"

Rereading this anecdote, I was newly impressed with Becca's description. For her, language not only defines and classifies experiences; it also endows them with poetic qualities. In Becca's description the puzzle pieces are correctly compared—the intellectual task—at the same time that they are given metaphoric names—the emotional response.

Again, I turn to the writing of Gordon Wells (1986) to document and emphasize the significance of this moment. "Making sense of an experience," writes Wells, "is . . . to a very great extent being able to construct a plausible story about it" (p. 196). As Becca explored the puzzle, a scenario began to take shape; in her narrative, each piece had a part to play. Wells describes such acts as central to life and learning: "Constructing stories in the mind—or *storying,* as it has been called—is one of the most fundamental means of making meaning; as such it is an activity that pervades all aspects of learning" (p. 194). More than anything else, this verbal system was created because of the human desire to savor as well as to shape experiences for oneself and, equally important, to share them with others. In our exchange, Becca highlighted some of the special qualities she saw in this bit of preschool paraphernalia. It is her view, her story, of how these puzzle pieces might be related to one another.

By the time children come to school they are experienced "storyers." In ways similar to Becca's puzzle scenario, they have been making sense of their world through the building of narratives that integrate their ever-increasing knowledge of how the world works. The school experience enhances the child's development by expanding his or her social and conceptual worlds. The child must make his or her way outside the familiar circle of family members. The reward is worth the effort—expanding contacts with the world bring expanding sources of information and differing perspectives. The classroom, by definition, provides opportunities for seeing what one child thinks in relation to what others think and is a powerful forum for moving youngsters along in their understanding of life experiences.

In this chapter, the three-year-old's recurring impulse to create narratives is examined in the context of school life. Classroom culture, the network of themes and shared experiences that bind a class group and make it unique, emerges from the interplay of children, adults, and activities. The vitality of that culture comes from the collaboration among teachers and children in designating and exploring their common interests. The impact of a program in which a class group evolves its own special themes and interests, its particular repertoire of shared narratives, makes the difference between a dull curriculum and one in which memorable teaching/learning moments are experienced by both children and adults.

SOCIAL PLAY

The young child's predilection for creating stories is encouraged in manifold ways in the nursery classroom. Indeed, the traditional setting provides house corners, block areas, and a variety of art materials and manipulative toys. These items all represent invitations to three-year-olds to weave stories of real and imagined worlds into their play.

One Monday morning in February, Christopher, true to his usual pattern, began his school day in the block corner. He was unusually proficient with the blocks. He tried and usually succeeded in producing a recognizable structure. This morning he produced his version of the Empire State Building. Because of its dramatic size and shape, this structure frequently sparks the building talents of many New York City preschoolers. Dan, working alongside Christopher, constructed a garage. Dan was not as thoroughly engaged in block play as Christopher, his special friend. Dan tended to pass the time in the block corner by keeping up a steady stream of conversation about the many events in his life that he wanted to share. While Christopher quietly and steadily put the blocks in place, Dan talked about his block garage, his father's garage, the bigness of Christopher's building, the police officer he met on his way to school, and so on. Christopher answered occasionally, but generally kept his eyes on his work. With the completion of his building, Christopher called me over—"Linda, look, the Empire State Building!"— and stood proudly beside his creation. I was appreciative. He then asked for a sign for his building. I told him to bring me the sign-making materials—a box with strips of paper and some magic markers. He did. He dictated and I wrote: "My Empire State Building—Do not knock it down. Christopher." Then Dan asked for a sign and he dictated: "This is my garage. Don't anybody touch it. Dan."

Next, the boys moved into the dress-up corner. In the fall, this area had been more or less constructed to suggest a home. It had a little stove, refrigerator, table and chairs, a doll's bed with dolls, and many kinds of clothes for dressing up. As the year went on, though, it was clear that the youngsters needed many different settings to support their narratives about life experiences; for example, a doctor's office, a restaurant, train stations, and airports. As a result I removed some of the furniture that defined the space as a home and added open-ended materials that could be transformed for any number of uses, such as large outdoor building blocks, wooden boards, and some cardboard blocks. The table and chairs were kept. Dress-up paraphernalia included vests, shirts, ties, knapsacks, dresses, colorful pieces of cloth, and hats of all kinds.

At this time in the year, Dan arrived almost everyday with new information regarding the jobs of police officers. He ordinarily incorporated the new material into his play of the day. Often he assumed his role as he entered the room and would stroll around the class in character for much of the work period. Sometimes he directed traffic; at other times he handed out tickets. On occasion he found an appropriate stick-like item to use as a baton as he "walked his beat."

This morning, similar to other mornings in recent weeks, the boys decided to convert the dress-up area into a police station. With my help, a police station was designed, complete with desks and signs. Dan's great delight and competence in exploring this theme communicated itself to many of the others who, though they had no clear sense of the purpose of certain actions, loved to sit at "desks" and work with the special papers and pens that had become standard equipment for the police station. The officers busied themselves marking the sheets that Dan called "tickets" and gave out to teachers and children as he moved about the room.

Recently, I had added a metal milk crate to the dramatic play equipment, and Dan was the first to find a use for it. "How about a jail?" he suggested to his companions. All agreed on this use. Dan turned the crate upside down so that it became escape-proof for all the stuffed animals that he incarcerated. The police officers then sat at their desks and guarded the criminals.

These dramatic play episodes are typical of the activities that young children choose to explore when provided with time, simple materials, and a setting that encourages this kind of play. Life experiences are recreated in scenes in which children play the principal roles and direct the action. Often when we take youngsters with us when we do our daily errands, they seem to be either in the way or not aware of what's going on. It requires only a few days in a school setting in which children are encouraged to explore and reenact familiar scenes to discover that they are very alert observers and can provide rather candid portraits of how adults behave in and out of the home.

The teacher's roles are provider of props, aider of organization ("Who is the Mommy for these babies?"), provider of reasons for actions ("It's cold outside so dress your babies warmly."), and provider of information about particular experiences ("Here is the menu where you can find the list of foods we cook in this restaurant."). In the last 20 years there has been a great deal of research documenting the importance of social play and its contribution to the child's learning about the world. Recently, social play has also been recognized as contributing to children's literacy learning. Such experiences, it has been demonstrated, expand young children's narrative skills and sharpen their grasp of story form (Galda, 1984). Indeed, the research suggests that social play should not be confined to nursery programs. Rather, it needs to be included in programs of primary-age children as well. In fact, the experiences that have been described above can be easily transformed to accommodate the story creations of children in the early grades. Learning, by definition, is making sense of experience. At the heart of this process is meaning making, or shaping the kaleidoscope of daily events into personal narratives.

TOMO AND THE PLAY–DOH

The following example of storytelling was recorded by Laura Guyther, one of the teachers working with Betsy Elliot. Laura had been sitting next to three-year-old Tomo at a table with Play-Doh. His story was spoken aloud and was meant to be shared with her. First he took a Play-Doh ball and patted it into a flat round shape. He used his finger to make appropriate marks for a face—eyes, nose, and mouth. He talked as he worked. Laura had witnessed Tomo's Play-Doh stories on other occasions and was fascinated by these personal narratives stimulated by his actions with the dough. This morning she came prepared to record Tomo's story. As the transcript reveals, Tomo placed himself at the center of the story. Sometimes he became a "friendly monster." At other moments, he became a bigger/older version of himself—"growing up" was connected to rolling the Play-Doh into a larger circle. At times he spoke in the monster's voice (indicated by italics).

> Friendly monster . . . I'm the same friendly monster . . . I'm still a baby . . . goodbye . . . I'm going to be much better . . . O.K. . . . yes . . . he's going to be bigger-bigger-bigger now . . . (rolls out the dough with a wooden roller—the action distorts the face and makes it bigger) . . . he's going to be four years old . . . the friendly monster is ready to come out . . . he's going to be his own self now, not his mother or his daddy . . . *Now I am four years old! Now I am four years old! Now I am four years old! I am big now. I am big now. I am big now. I can jump up! Hello! I'm the same monster. Goodbye! Goodbye!* . . . (To Laura as he rolls out the Play-Doh even further) He was much bigger, right? He's going to get bigger, bigger than you. . . . Then he's going to be daddy. . . . He does grow up. . . . See? I'm the same monster (rolls the clay face up Laura's arm) Goodbye . . . see you next morning. . . . See, he's going to be bigger now. . . . See, he's a daddy now (rolls out the dough so that face is even larger and again rolls it up Laura's arm) See? still I can roll up . . . I'm the same monster now. . . . Goodbye, see you next day . . . I'm going to be a daddy now. (Tomo continues to play, but Laura needs to turn her attention to other children at the table.)

During these few moments, an entire life story was enacted with a small ball of Play-Doh. Tomo contemplated real as well as imagined roles in life. He went from being a baby—the Play-Doh was correspondingly small—to a boy-monster who turned four. Such an age represents a milestone in a three-year-old's life. He continued to grow and assumed the role of a daddy. He even said things a daddy might say ("Goodbye, see you next morning"). A characteristic style of social play for Tomo was through the simultaneous engagement with the Play-Doh, his story, and his teacher as listener. Such a feat is typical of three-year-olds whose unique abilities transform any setting into a medium for creating stories. As youngsters mature, they slowly become more self-conscious and deliberate about separating their social play from other experiences.

STORY DRAMA

In Vivian Gussin Paley's wonderful book, *Mollie Is Three* (1986), three-year-olds experiences in social play are highlighted in a unique fashion. With an ever-present tape recorder, Paley captured children's dialogues at the easel, in their group drama sessions (described below), and especially in dictated stories. In her class of three-, four-, and five-year olds, she focuses on the youngest children and records their efforts to come to terms with life experiences—problems or "scary" things—through their stories.

> Place [the] three-year-old in a room with other threes, and sooner or later they will become an acting company. Should there happen to be a number of somewhat older peers about to offer stage directions and dialogue, the metamorphosis will come sooner rather than later. The dramatic images that flutter through their minds, as so many unbound stream-of-consciousness novels, begin to emerge as audible scripts to be performed on demand. (p. xiv)

With these words, Paley described for the reader a major program theme for her nursery youngsters. Stories that they create, their "novels" about their life experiences, are written down and then acted out at a later time. This procedure, so successful for many teachers in dramatizing favorite storybooks, has been significantly expanded by Paley through her use of children's stories as the scripts. As the title suggests, Paley's book highlights Mollie's growth and development through storying in her first year of classroom life. The following dialogue between Mollie (M) and Paley (P) reveals the collaborative quality of the creation of one of Mollie's first stories (p. 17):

M: The bad guy and the red horse.
P: Is that the whole story, Mollie?
M: And a girl.
P: Does she have a name?
M: No name of girl. No name. The ghost is there. There *is* a girl. A ghost and a girl.
P: Does the girl do something?
M: She makes pies something and the ghost gets her pies. Then the ghost takes it away to the gorilla's house and he was very sad. And he never saw the pies again. Don't tell anyone.

After Mollie finished her story, Paley writes, she left the story table. She returned a few minutes later to announce that she was going to be the ghost and Frederick was going to be the gorilla. What Mollie had in mind was that when the class had their daily time for story dramas, she wanted to act out her story. Though she had watched other children do this, this was the first time she had requested that her story be acted out. This is not surprising since it was still the beginning of the year and Mollie, as one of the three's, was just beginning to feel comfortable with her new surroundings and with the idea of contributing to this major group event (p. 18).

[Paley continues,] "Mollie has decided to act out today's story. The others, she said, were too scary."

"Is this one scary?" Frederick is always first to ask the question.

Mollie gives a "scary" look. "Everyone will get scared today," she warns.

I begin Mollie's story. "The bad guy and the red horse, and a girl. No name of girl. No name. The ghost is there. There *is* is a girl. A ghost and a girl. She makes pies something and the ghost gets her pies. . . ."

"Gimme back those pies!" Libby shouts. "Say that, Mollie." The children's stories are part of the unfolding culture of the group and, as in play, members of the audience feel they have the right to influence the outcome.

"Say it, Mollie," Libby persists.

Mollie imitates the older girl, then adds a new line of her own. "Gimme those pies! And the ghost gobbles it up too fast!" She stuffs her fingers into her mouth and slurps noisily. "Everybody watch me do this. It's not too scary for you now."

As Mollie's story ended, Paley reported, everyone was watching her and participating in her narrative. Paley noted as well that the interaging of her class group had the effect of stimulating the younger children to participate in this fairly sophisticated class event earlier in the year than they would ordinarily if the group consisted solely of three-year-olds.

The simplicity of Paley's procedures is especially noteworthy. She acted as narrator and provided a faithful rendition of the story Mollie dictated earlier. The excitement of the story was immediately sensed by the children, especially Libby, who was prompted to make a contribution to the drama. This vignette provides us with a vivid reminder of how little it takes to stimulate children's imaginations. Mollie sat in the middle of the group, her teacher read her story, and everyone was transported to her imagined world.

In another section of the book, Paley reported on three-year-old Frederick's first experience with having his story acted out. The text was "Frederick"; that was all (p. 12).

I hold up Frederick's page and read, "Frederick." He runs to the center of the rug and smiles. The others, seated on low benches against the walls, smile back but I yield to the teacher's role.

"Is anything different about Frederick's story?" I ask.

"Because he's Frederick," Libby answers.

"Right. But I wondered about a story that has only one word."

John, nearly five, responds quickly. "It's not one word. It's one person."

In this vignette, Paley captured a wonderful example of some of the differences between adults' and children's understanding of stories. For adults, a "proper" narrative should have more than one word. Children, however, don't count words. Rather they respond to meanings, and most words, certainly most names, express much meaning. As usual, Paley was quick to pick up on the implications of this episode. She writes: "Of course, a person *is* a story. Frederick need not do something to justify his presence in the story" (p. 12).

In these short excerpts from her book, Paley reveals herself as an excellent model of a teacher collaborating with children. In her dialogues with children, we see an adult who very deliberately and conscientiously attempts to see things from the child's perspective. Since she feels social play is of critical value to the development of the nursery schooler, she uses this frame to guide many of her interactions. She suggests roles and pushes children to elaborate their thoughts and feelings; inevitably she leads youngsters in the direction of dictating as well as acting out their stories. For her, the noting of special themes that seem to fascinate each of her children is a constant activity. As she interacts with youngsters, she is continually documenting for herself the broad life themes that individual children are struggling to understand. Children, of course, sense what it is their teachers value and will move in the directions adults favor. In Paley's classroom, children know that their stories are valued and that problems they may share in their exchanges with their teacher will be duly noted. This is enough to stimulate youngsters to use story dramas as a medium for growth in understanding themselves, their peers, and the creation of imaginative realms of existence.

RHYMES AND STORIES

At the beginning of my year teaching three-year-olds, I assumed that they, being born in the last quarter of the twentieth century, might find the traditional rhyme repertoire unappealing. I was wrong. Within the first two weeks, I realized that in this school year, traditional rhymes would form the major source of our poetic play. I learned that most of them knew and could repeat with gusto "Jack and Jill," "Mary Had a Little Lamb," "Humpty Dumpty," and many others. I saw, too, that repetition was the way it should be done. If we said them once, we said them dozens of times without any diminishing of enthusiasm. Also, and this was most important, I discovered that any attempts I might make to obscure rather than emphasize the repetitious sing-song cadences were not appreciated. The rhythm of the four-beat couplet, I found, might be exaggerated but not obscured.

In the rhyme repetitions, these three-year-olds were examining—and practicing—the sound patterns of their language. Sound is the sensory aspect of speech; it is the tangible attribute of the system that children love to manipulate as they explore the musicality of their language. The force of the group's interest in traditional verses led me to end each morning with a group gathering called, appropriately, "Rhyme Time." In fact, their interest matched my own. I was just completing my doctoral work on elementary children's wordplay and was keenly interested in the kinds of verbal play that fascinated younger children. Sound play through rhymes, it was clear, was a major area of experimentation.

In the course of the year, we developed an oral repertoire of 30 to 40 favorite verses, including many songs. While Paley's program was characterized by the exploration of story dramas, one of the primary aspects of my program was the exploration of rhymes. And just as Paley's youngsters looked forward to the sharing of their stories through drama, mine anticipated "Rhyme Time" each morning. They began to make up their own rhymes or they requested that something be said or read.

After exploring traditional examples of the rhyme repertoire, I began to search for other verses to learn. At Rhyme Time one morning I read a selection from a picture book of game chants and rhymes popular with the primary ages.

> Way down South where bananas grow,
> A grasshopper stepped on an elephant's toe.
> The elephant said, with tears in his eyes,
> "Pick on somebody your own size."

When I finished, the serious expression on everyone's face told me that the choice had not been a good one. Conceptually unable to appreciate the humor of the verse, these three-year-olds appeared to identify with the plight of the elephant. I turned to other pages and read other selections with more success. At this point, though, I began to see that there were disadvantages to using a picture book. These youngsters tended to come from homes where storybook reading was a regular family activity. In the school setting, most enjoyed listening to a story and following the pictures, as long as the selection was not too long. Unlike the repeating of rhymes from memory, where the focus was on the words and their sounds, the use of the book proved to be distracting because of the added visual stimulus. The children no longer even attempted to say the words with me as they carefully scrutinized the pictures on each page. After one more attempt to read rhymes to the group, I decided that our Rhyme Times would be used for exploring verse without books. As a result, I needed to expand my memorized repertoire of verses in order to expand that of my group.

In the middle of the school year, I began to record stories they were telling about their drawings and paintings. One morning, as Kimberly sat engrossed with crayons and paper, I invited her to tell me her story. She began: "Shama sheema/Mash day 'n' pash day . . ." Though I expected a narrative, I realized (in time) that this poetic rendition of sounds was, indeed, a story worth recording. I wrote as she continued.

'N' mash day 'n' cash day
'N' mash day 'n' mush day
'N' mush day 'n' push day
'N' lush day 'n' push day.

At Rhyme Time, I read Kimberly's creation to the class. They listened with rapt attention. Someone asked that I "do it again." I did. At Rhyme Time the next day, Evelyn asked for Kimberly's rhyme story. I read it many times during the next weeks, and soon everybody began to say it with me. Subsequently, Nikki, among others, was prompted to produce a similar story. This was also recorded and read to the class.

Daz day 'n' daz day
'N' maz day 'n' maz day
'N' muz day 'n' laz day
'N' saz day.

Like Kimberly, Nikki was experimenting with substituting initial phonemes and repeating the same words in rhythmical sequence. A year later, Nikki, now four, greeted me after a long absence with "Hi, Linda . . . Binda, Minda, Cinda." That this kind of play is a favorite for these ages is not surprising when we consider that it uses the most popular rhyme form in children's traditional verses. Then, too, I think just seeing me again stirred memories of some of the many good times our group spent together regaling ourselves by repeating our favorite rhymes.

Particular teacher interests provide an important starting point for designing a program. If it happens, as it did in Paley's and my classes, that these interests are shared by the group, then the way is set for the collaborative design and exploration of curriculum. When this kind of intersection of interests takes place, it contributes enormously to the development of the sense of belonging, the feeling that children and adults in a particular class group share something unique. In short, it helps to shape classroom culture. What cannot be replicated in the classroom is the intimacy of the one-on-one interactions that define family exchanges and contribute so much to molding connections among family members. However, the sense of belonging, of sharing something special, can and must find its way into school life. After all, it is largely through sharing pleasurable activities with teachers and peers that children form strong connections to people beyond their family group.

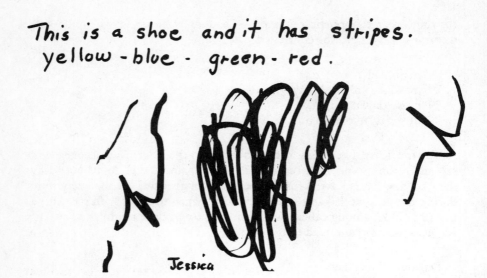

This is a shoe and it has stripes. yellow - blue - green - red.

Jessica

Figure 5.1   *Jessica's "sneaker" story*

The rhymes were only part of an ever-increasing repertoire that I recorded and read at Rhyme Time. These stories varied enormously in content and form. Some were very much related to the here and now. Such was the case with one of the stories Jessica created (Figure 5.1). She stared at her colorful new sneakers when asked to tell her story about her picture, a simple rendering of lines made by magic markers that matched the colors in her new sneakers. Her story: "This is a shoe and it has stripes. Yellow-green-blue-red." Every time we read the story at Rhyme Time, Jessica would check her feet and, if she had her sneakers on, she would obligingly hold one foot up while her story was read.

Jonathan created a story as he made marks on the page—a gestural picture story (Figure 5.2). Jonathan's story: "A bee monster [one circle]. This is a caterpillar monster, too . . . [more connected circles] and a snake monster [never raised marker so that circles looked like a coiled snake] . . . [lifted marker and made dots] And how about a mosquito?" I recorded what Jonathan said and then we taped the picture with words to a piece of construction paper and put it in the children's story box, a special container for their creations.

Becca's interest had turned to fairy tales. As she told her story she pointed to each "character" in the picture she was in the process of creating (Figure 5.3): "A little princess is walking by and here is a dragon and the princess got the dragon and the fairy godfather got the bad dragon and the little girl

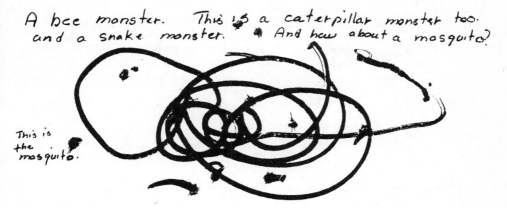

Figure 5.2 Jonathan's "gestural" story

and the princess lived happily ever after." She had begun to adopt common fairy tale phrases as she created her own versions of the dramatic plots.

To ask three-year-olds to repeat or revise what has been produced would be to intrude upon the process. Either we get it the first time or not at all. Their creations represent a blend of story structures, book language, and experimentation with words, and, like the nonsense rhymes, they are suffused with rhythm and repetition. Here are five more examples:

JUDITH AND THE RAIN
I love the rain coming down
Because I love when it makes the drips
They make too much music.

LIAM AND THE SNOW
It's snow. We can't go outside.
See the big pieces are falling.
Ping! Bong! Pup pup bu bu bup! Peter popper.
It's snowing out!
I'm gonna taste those big pieces when I get out there.

TOMMY'S VISIT TO UNCLE JACK'S
It was on Sunday. We went on the train first. And then we took a bus and Uncle Jack picked us up at the bus station. We played and played and played. And we sleep and sleep and sleep for many days. We picked strawberries by the field. Then we had a whole bunch. We took them for lunch.

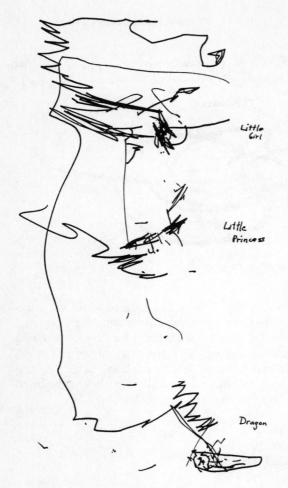

Little
Girl

Little
Princess

Dragon

Figure 5.3
Becca's version
of a fairy tale

A little princess is walking by
and here is a dragon and the
princess got the dragon and the fairy god father
got the bad dragon and the little girl
and the princess lived happily after.

The End

Becca

EDITH'S VISIT TO THE DOCTOR
I whined when he put that stick in my mouth.
I whined, whined, whined.
I laughed when it was over.

EMILY'S STORY
It's really a grown-up song but I'm writing it. This is a princess who's waiting for her lawyer to come back from France. And the lawyer never came back. The lawyer was thinking about the princess . . . And the lawyer came back to the princess.

These selections reveal the authors' exploration of narrative form along with verbal art. They are getting the information across (going to the doctor) at the same time that they give it an expressive rendering ("I whined, whined, whined"). And it is the expressive qualities that are most fully brought out through wordplay, that is, elaboration for its own sake rather then the simple imparting of facts.

Though at first these recordings of children's language were shared solely with the group, eventually I put together a class book that included a sample from each child's work and made a copy for each to take home. I also made copies of our rhyme repertoire for my students' parents and encouraged them to repeat the rhymes with their youngsters. It is especially important to involve parents in the appreciation of children's efforts at creating stories as well as their love of rhyme. Parents and caregivers, as noted, are key people in children's education, and they are much more able to contribute appropriately to their youngsters' developed abilities if they understand the significance of these beginning efforts.

CLASSROOM CULTURE

As children move between oral renditions of life as they understand it and versions of their experience dictated to their teacher, they slowly expand their perspectives of family, school, and community—their mental model of their social world. Their stories express what they understand as the important views and values of the significant people in their lives. As they create their narratives, children examine the hopes and fears, the things that excite as well as sadden the people they care about.

Not only in our cities, but throughout our country, class groups are made up of youngsters who come from different countries, who may speak a language other than English, and who are, in part, products of a heritage that differs from that of their classmates. Within this diversity, however, certain universal experiences prevail and shape a class group. The fact that youngsters share a common social community beyond their family culture, the fact that youngsters share with each other the impulse to make sense of their experiences through storying, and the fact that they share the same classroom in which they are contributors to the shaping of class life—these are the threads out of which teachers and children weave a unique and sustaining social community. Within this frame, differences among youngsters are celebrated and given a prominent place in the spontaneous as well as deliberate telling and retelling of personal narratives. One child's experiences are juxtaposed to another's as children come to know how they are alike and how they differ.

In a very real sense, the classroom is the center of the process by which our country continues to shape a shared heritage from its diverse social and cultural roots. Each school year in which a new constellation of students and teachers set out to live together offers a setting within which a unique social and cultural group develops and crystallizes around the shared interests of its members. In Paley's classroom a binding experience was the creating of story dramas; in mine, it was the presence of language play and the resulting exploration of the rhyme repertoire. In both classrooms, these program themes, given the momentum of teacher and child interest, found their way into the daily schedule of events. Paley had her regular story drama sessions, and my class ended the half-day with Rhyme time.

Storying is a natural focus in classrooms that make use of children's differing experiences and perspectives for building a program. As noted, all youngsters possess the impulse to make sense of their experiences in any way they can, and storying, as Wells (1986) put it, is as connected to human experience as breathing. And it is these impulses that class programs must build upon as they bring youngsters along in their language and literacy development. The composing of narratives, whether in social play or on one's own, needs to be at the heart of the three-year-old program—indeed, it needs to be in programs for every early childhood and elementary age group. Creating narratives challenges those who are experienced at storying to expand their competence, at the same time that it fills a gap for those who may need more experience with composing. Sharing the narratives helps to build an appreciation of life's variety in this generation of children who must learn to live in communities whose cultures are shaped as much by change as by permanence.

What is not included in this chapter is the other side of the coin of the child's development of a sense of story—that is, the reading and sharing of storybooks. Indeed, becoming familiar with the world of storybooks and creating narratives are inseparable developments. The two activities reinforce one another; exposure to literature helps youngsters to identify narrative structures, which are then integrated into their own compositions. Chapter 6 examines the story-reading program in one three-year-old classroom and documents the significance of such a program to the continuing literacy development of the young child.

6

Storytime Talk
Exploring Narrative Form

Louise Crowe's class of sixteen three-year-olds had just come in from the play yard. The children hung up their coats and took seats at one of two tables where they have their morning snack. The children filled the waiting time by taking a book to look at from the book basket on each table. They looked forward to this moment and were discriminating in their book choices. Some could be heard repeating a story to themselves as they turned the pages. Others scrutinized the illustrations carefully, reading the pictured events. One little girl found a torn page, which she immediately reported. Within minutes, Louise repaired the page with the roll of tape she kept in the book basket for that purpose. Two youngsters shared a book with pictures of boats. As they turned the pages they argued about what kinds of boats were represented and what the boats were doing. They seemed to enjoy disagreeing with each other.

What was clear to any observer was that these youngsters came from book-oriented families. Like Robyn and Giti, most brought to their school experience many pleasurable home experiences sharing books with favorite adults or older siblings. Book-handling skills, reading and interpreting pictures, or telling and retelling stories were already a part of most of these youngsters' reading repertoire.

It was not surprising, then, that these three's were especially well prepared to participate in the daily story-reading sessions that took place during the morning rest time. With the help of Louise and her two assistants, the children cleaned up from work time, got their blankets out of their cubbies, spread them on one of two rugs in the room, and settled down for a story. To make the setting as intimate as possible, the group was divided in half—eight youngsters with one teacher and eight with another.

AN EXPERIENCE IN STORY READING

What follows is a transcription from a videotape of Louise reading *Are You My Mother?* by P. D. Eastman (1960) to half of the group on a morning in early December. To signal the children that story reading was about to begin, Louise held up the book and asked if anyone had heard it before. From the nearly unanimous responses of "Yes" and "Yaaaayyy," it appeared that all the children were familiar with the book. Though Louise had not yet read it to this class, it had apparently been a part of their story-reading experiences outside of school. Eastman's book was originally written for primary-age children as a beginner reader, but it has become very popular with younger children—toddlers (like Robyn) as well as three- and four-year-olds. Not a simple text, the story is built around some relatively complex narrative structures, which even older children might have a difficult time fully comprehending. In the transcription of Louise's story session, it is clear that, despite the familiarity and the pleasure these three's take in the story, they have yet to grasp the key narrative structures on which the story is constructed. The videotape of this session reveals the confrontation between text and listeners, with the latter struggling to extend their understanding of life as it is represented in the world of fiction. The transcription underscores Louise's role in helping the children to make sense of the story through her talking and questioning as she reads (Cochran-Smith, 1984, 1986).

The World of Fiction

As Louise began reading, the children immediately became attentive. After reading the text on a page, Louise turned the book around and showed the picture to the group. It was generally during these moments that conversations took place. In the transcriptions below and on the following pages, the column to the left of the dialogue identifies the purpose of Louise's questions and comments. In the dialogue, italics indicate book text (Eastman, 1960, pp. 3–10, 12–19, 20, 44–63).

	LOUISE: *A mother bird sat on her nest. The egg jumped. "Oh, oh," said the mother bird, "My baby will be here. He will want to eat."*
Focusing attention through question.	(Shows the picture to the group) What does she mean, her baby will be here?
	JEFFREY: (Looking at the picture) A dog.
	LOUISE: A dog? *"I must get something for my baby bird to eat. I'll be back." And away she went.*

Reminding listener of appropriate behavior.	Alexis, turn around so you can see the pictures. *The egg jumped and jumped and jumped and jumped and out of the egg came the baby bird.* (Shows pictures) Can you see it? Can you see the baby bird, Alexis?
Annotating the text.	*"Where is my mother?" he said.* He was just born and he doesn't see his mother.

Observing the effortless way in which most of these youngsters tuned into this fictional framework, I was reminded of how much learning about books preceded this particular story experience. As noted, what has been learned is that books create an "autonomous fictional world" (Snow & Ninio, 1986, p. 135). Pictures and text go together to tell of an event that exists outside of daily experience. The time and place of this world have their own dimensions and often mix life-as-it-is with life-as-it-might-be. In children's books, mother animals tend to be similar to human mothers; they often talk and wear clothes. The rapt attention of these three-year-olds bore testimony to the strength of the storybook experience. For these youngsters, the experience was a moment in which to participate, vicariously, in the plight of a small creature. One sensed that during the story reading, the images evoked by the text were as real to the children as life itself.

In this opening sequence, key plot elements were introduced. First, the mother determined that she must gather food for her soon-to-be-born baby. After she departed, the baby bird did, indeed, arrive and was puzzled by the absence of his mother. Louise highlighted the first action with a question (What does she mean, "her baby will be here?") and the second with an explanatory comment (He was just born and he doesn't see his mother.). In traditional nursery classrooms, Marilyn Cochran-Smith (1984, 1986) notes, story reading is an extension of family book sharing. The main reason for reading is the pleasure of sharing the experience. Further, in both home and nursery school situations, the adults are guided by their sense of what will make the story fully comprehensible to young listeners. Hence, they often pause and annotate, or expand, the text with questions and comments designed to focus the listeners' attention on key events and actions.

Of utmost importance to the child's grasp of the nature of the fictional world is the understanding of its relationship to the real world. Though the fictional world exists only in the imagination, it is to be responded to emotionally, and, to a lesser extent, logically, as if it were an extension of life. When Louise asked her listeners to interpret the mother bird's action, she was signaling them that their personal experiences are an appropriate source for understanding this character. In Cochran-Smith's (1984) terms, this kind of teacher annotation comes under the general heading of "life-to-text interactions" (p. 174) and represents a significant way in which readers must actively respond to and evaluate text material. Even though Louise's questions did not elicit any responses, just the asking models this important reader response to text. In other words, reading is partly the adoption of a questioning attitude toward story content and the continual searching for its meaning.

Louise also underscored the baby bird's dilemma by emphasizing the unusualness of a newborn being separated from its mother. Again her focus was on how the baby bird's experience was similar to the human one. Her emphasis on this point helped to highlight the central action of the story, namely, the baby bird's search for its mother.

Life as Development

Louise did not comment on the distinctly unhuman-like characteristic of a newborn being not only aware but also articulate about its mother's absence. Such supra-human characteristics suggest that the baby bird is connected to the mythological world where creatures tend to begin existence fully formed and fully conscious. The baby bird's origins, however, prove to be multi-faceted. It is revealed that, despite his precociousness, he is subject to human laws of growth and development. The next sequence reveals how Louise explores this perspective of life with the group.

	LOUISE: *But he looked up, he doesn't see her, and he looked down and he doesn't see her. "I will go to look for her." So away he went and he stepped out of his nest. Down out of the tree he went.*
Illustration moves plot ahead.	(Pointing to picture of the baby bird falling to the ground) What happened to him? What happened here?
	JEFFREY: He falled.
	LOUISE: Why did he fall?
	JEFFREY: Because he was, he was (mumbles).
	LOUISE: He was what?
	JEFFREY: (mumbles something about biting) An' den an' den he felled down.
	LOUISE: He sure did. *Down, down, down, down and it was a long way down. The baby bird could not fly.*

Life-to-text connection.	I thought baby birds knew how to fly. How come he couldn't fly?
	JEFFREY: Birds do.
	LOUISE: How come this baby bird couldn't fly?
	JEFFREY: 'Cause he mudder (mumbles)
	AUGUSTA: He couldn't fly yet because he was a baby.
	LOUISE: Oh, you think he hadn't learned how, yet? I guess he hadn't learned yet. But you know what? (Shifting to text) *He could walk. "Now I will go and find her," he said.*
Text-to-life connection.	AUGUSTA: My brother can walk.
	LOUISE: Your brother can walk?
	AUGUSTA: An' he could an' he could talk.
	LOUISE: And he's learning to talk, yeah.

Though a remarkably conscious creature, then, our baby bird is not able to fly. Louise commented on this inconsistency with bird characteristics ("I thought baby birds knew how to fly") and followed it with a question ("How come he couldn't fly?"). Again, the message was that in this fictional world we can expect very clear connections to life as we know it. It means that lfe experiences must be constantly reviewed to find those that might be useful for interpreting text. That life develops and that immature beings must learn things like locomotion skills is an experience shared by most of the biological world. Certainly, in our human world, the developmental view of life is a major standard by which we describe and document our progress from birth to death. We are especially observant of the growth stages of our young; we note with pleasure and pride their progress from babbling to talking or from being cradled to walking.

Augusta was quick to follow Louise's conversational focus. She articulated the developmental perspective by pointing out that the bird was just a baby. Louise was low-keyed rather than emphatic in her confirmation of Augusta's explanation. She commented on the fact that this was Augusta's opinion ("Oh, you think . . .") and then she suggested that she, too, tended to hold the view ("I guess he hadn't learned yet.") For Louise to be too emphatic would imply that text interpretations belong to the category of factual, right/wrong responses—which they don't. Text interpretations should be treated almost without exception as personal observations, an opportunity for listeners to reflect about story events, and to dialogue with one another, or with the author—via the text—about meanings represented in the narrative. What separates literature from more didactic views of life is its open-ended relation to experience. Writers intend that meanings will be interpreted according to their readers' personal experience; it is in this way that they engage their audience in an exchange of views.

Augusta capped this conversation with comments about the walking/talking developments of her baby brother. Clearly, her current family experience stimulated these text-to-life connections and made her especially aware of the developmental view of things.

Plot Machinery

The baby bird began to look for his mother, but since he had never seen her he did not who, or what, to look for.

	LOUISE: *He didn't know what his mother looked like.*
Life-to-text (How are we the same/different from this character?)	How come he didn't know what his mother looked like? You know what your mother looks like. (Holding up the picture showing the baby bird walking along in the distance and the mother bird in the foreground pulling up a worm)
	SAM: (Looking intently at the picture as he crawls toward it and points to the mother) I think . . . I think . . . the mother is pulling up a worm. (Says more that is unintelligible)
	LOUISE: Ohhh, Sam says this is his mother pulling up a worm to take to him. (Jeffrey plants himself in front of the book, blocking the view of the other children.) Go back, Jeffrey.
	SAM: And the mother worm, I mean, the bird mom, thinks that the baby's in the nest.
	LOUISE: Oh, yeah, she doesn't know he's out looking for her. You're right, Sam. I bet the mother thinks that the bird is still up in the nest just waiting for her to get back.
	SAM: But he isn't!
	LOUISE: He's not . . .

| Revising and expanding text for greater clarity. | Well, since he didn't know what his mother looked like, he didn't know that was his mother. (Shifts to text) *He just walked right past her.* |

Louise attempted to begin a discussion regarding the baby bird's lack of recognition of his mother with a question: "How come he didn't know what his mother looked like?" And, as she did above, she guided her listeners to search their experience with their mothers as a way of understanding the baby bird's dilemma: "You know what your mother looks like." Her tone suggested the ridiculousness of the possibility that they might not know what their mothers looked like. She appeared to be looking for the reasonable inference, one that is consistent with real life experience—that because the baby bird had never seen his mother, he wouldn't be able to recognize her. Louise's comment was followed by a pause. The idea of being aware of someone—someone as significant as a mother—whom they could not visually recognize appeared to be entirely beyond the experience of these youngsters. Indeed, it is beyond the experience of most of us and cannot be easily explained through the use of the life-to-text category of analysis. What we are confronting, in fact, is a common plot device in which characters related in some significant way cross one another's paths without recognizing one another. Explanations, as a result, need to come more from a perusal of other stories rather than from the use of the life-to-text perspective. Text-to-text comparisons involve a more abstract level of analysis which requires the ability to sift through one's literary repertoire and to search for similarities and differences among stories. To make such comparisons presumes a longer and more extensive acquaintance with stories and plot mechanisms than most three's are likely to possess.

Sam, fortunately, moved in another direction. Wisely, Louise followed his lead. He examined the picture very carefully. Mother bird was in the foreground (busy pulling a worm out of the ground) and was unaware of the proximity of her baby, shown walking in the background. Sam made the connection that the worm was food for the baby, the reason the mother bird left the nest in the first place. Further, he deduced that the mother bird no doubt thought that her baby was safe in the nest, the implication being that if this was so, she wouldn't have to pay much attention to who was walking by. Sam ignored the question of recognition and explained the missed connection by using those life-to-text inferences that could be supported by the story context and the illustration. Louise continued to explore the possibilities that Sam suggested and agreed that the unsuspecting mother probably thought that her baby was in the nest. Enjoying the deception, Sam declared, "But he isn't!"

In terms of storytime talk, the exchange between Louise and Sam was significant for a number of reasons. Asking questions that often turn out to be more complex than is immediately understood happens all the time in the classroom. In fact, it happens more often in classrooms in which teachers solicit conversations about story structures than those in which discussions tend to center on fill-in-the-blank type exchanges; for example, "What does the mother have in her mouth?" "A worm."/ "Does she see the baby bird?" "No."/ "Does he see her?" "No." These kinds of labeling and picture-reading episodes do have a place in story conversations. They can be especially important with less-experienced story listeners who may not be familiar with how to approach pictured events. However, when they make up most of the storytime talk, then opportunities for the development of children's grasp of narrative structures are short circuited. In classrooms where the teacher has indicated that story reading is a time for negotiating story meanings, children tend to provide feedback, either by their silence or, as Sam did, by moving in a direction that makes sense to them. In the above exchange, the way was left open for Sam to lead the conversation and, in good collaborative style, to help Louise understand the perspective of at least one of her listeners.

Recognition Scene

The baby bird's search for his mother provided most of the rest of the action that, in literary terms, followed the repetitive pattern. He repeated the question, "Are you my mother?" to everyone (cat, dog, cow) and everything (car, boat, plane) he met. Though continually rebuffed, the bird was persistent in his quest. Finally he encountered a "big thing."

	LOUISE: *Just then the baby bird saw a big thing. This must be his mother. "There she is, there she is, there's my mother," he called.* (Pointing to "the thing" in the picture)
Life-to-text/Identifying the "big thing."	What did he see?
	AUGUSTA: It's not his mother.
	ANOTHER CHILD: It's not his mother.
	LOUISE: It's not his mother? What does it look like?
	CHILD: Like a toy.
	LOUISE: You've seen a toy like that?
	CHILD: It's a dump truck.
	LOUISE: It's something that lifts up dirt in a big shovel.
	CHILD: It's a crane.

LOUISE: Like a crane.

CHILD: A crane.

LOUISE: Right. *And he ran right up to it. "Mother, mother, here I am," he said. But the big thing just said, "SNORT!"*

CHILD: "Snort?"

LOUISE: *"Oh, you're not my mother," said the baby bird. "You're a snort! I have to get out of here." But the baby bird cannot get away. The snort went up. It went way, way up. And up, up, up went the baby bird*

Transposing text for clarification.

because it was on the shovel of the snort, the crane. *But where was the snort going?*

CHILD: His home.

LOUISE: *"Oh, oh, what's the snort going to do to me? Get me out of here," said the baby bird.*

Predicting plot.

CHILD: He's going to take him home.

LOUISE: You think so? *Just then the snort came to a stop. "Where am I? Where am I?" said the baby bird. "I wanna go home. I want my mother." And then something happened. The snort put that baby bird right back in the tree. The baby bird was home. Just then the mother bird came back to the tree. "Do you know who I am?" she said to her baby.*

Confirming Sam's inference.

(Pointing to the picture) She brought him a worm.

"Yes, I know who you are. You're not a kitten. You're not a hen. You're not a dog. You're not a cow. You're not a boat, or a plane, or a snort! You are a bird. You are my mother!"

Text-to-life (Mother birds are like human mothers.)

JEFFREY: (Pointing to the picture) An' ders his Mudder . . . An' de mommy's hugging him.

LOUISE: The mommy looks like she has her wing over him. That's her way of hugging him.

CHILD: Read another one.

After a discussion around the identification of the "big thing," Louise read straight through to the end of the text. The "big thing," it turned out, was strategically placed and was able to return the baby bird to his nest. This bit of *deus ex machina* was perfectly understandable within the framework of a fictional world. Remarkable and fantastic happenings of this type often provide plot twists and resolutions in stories for children and adults.

The recognition scene followed as the mother returned and innocently asked, "Do you know who I am?" The baby bird needed no further prodding to enumerate names of creatures he knew she was not; he capped the list with the announcement that not only did he know she was his mother, but he also knew that she was a bird. We were not told what prompted the baby bird's sudden recognition of his mother. For this group, however, such a plot gap was of little consequence, since they had difficulty comprehending the baby bird's lack of recognition of its mother. That mother and baby were reunited was the significant and fitting resolution of this story for these listeners. And, as Jeffrey commented, the mother bird, like human mothers, was tender and loving in this moment as she hugged her baby.

What becomes particularly clear in this transcription of *Are You My Mother?* is that understanding narrative form is a complex task, which can only evolve out of many experiences with books. It is not just a matter of understanding that a story has a beginning, middle, and end, or that animals can assume human characteristics. Rather, it is a matter of becoming conversant with those narrative structures that have been a part of the world of literature for centuries. Even in this supposedly simple story, the author used plot devices that were abstract and that could be comprehended by young listeners only after many readings. As noted, though this book appeared to be familiar to most of these youngsters, they were still engaged in the process of making sense of certain narrative devices. Hence, rereading favorite books is also a significant factor in supporting and extending children's developing grasp of narrative form.

IMPLICATIONS FOR EARLY LITERACY PROGRAMS

Traditionally, the early and middle grades have an emphasis on programs for learning to read and write. First grade was the magical year in which children would take those first steps toward independent reading. What has not been adequately understood is the significance of all the learning that precedes those steps, that is, the crucial relationship between emergent literacy and learning to read and write. In most of the educational world, the impact of nursery programs on literacy learning has yet to be understood. Storytimes and story dictations are "nice," but not "necessary," many parents and teachers say, not the "real stuff" of teaching reading and writing. Still captives of reading myths, they believe that literacy teaching and learning can only be done with formal materials and at a certain age.

To be consistent with our expanded definition of what reading is and how and when it is learned, we need to give up these myths and to revise our views of school literacy programs. The descriptions in this chapter of selected programs for three year olds have revealed that instead of a simple "preparation" for the beginning of real learning, early childhood programs provide critical experiences in the child's language development. Storytimes provide moments in which teachers and children actively engage in reading/listening and dialoguing about books. Such a program is an inescapable part of what it means to join the ranks of readers. Similarly, learning to compose and write must engage children right from the start in the active process of composing narratives about their life experiences, including their literary experiences. These can be shared orally or they can be recorded and reread at future times.

Finally, these descriptions provide us with portraits of teachers who have adopted collaborative methods in their work with children. Developing story sense with three-year-olds needs to be accomplished indirectly, by questions and comments designed to elicit children's active interaction with literature or by the composing of their own narratives. Further, the pleasure of the experience as well as the engagement of the listeners must never take a back seat to formal and didactic methods of teaching. Collaboration, we know, implies the capacity on the part of the teacher to respond sensitively to children's questions and to adopt the children's perspectives of things—in brief, to have sufficient confidence in themselves and in children to know not only when to lead but also when to follow. This kind of approach must permeate literacy teaching/learning in all of the early childhood and elementary years. The ubiquitousness of the more formal teaching methods makes the adoption of this approach difficult even for teachers who want to implement it. The myth that teaching is telling dies hard in all of us, especially when it comes to teaching reading. In short, with the recognition of the significance of emergent literacy programs, we need to beware of the impulse to distort the process by designing story-reading or story-writing formulas and prescriptions for nursery classrooms.

Our most powerful motivation, though, for revising our approach should be our consideration for our young students. The three-year-olds who have been a part of the class programs described above are well on their way to joining the ranks of the literate. Let's speculate about their future in terms of the literacy programs they are likely to encounter in the next few years. Assuming the continuation of programs for story listening and story composing in their four- and five-year-old classes, by the time these youngsters reach first grade, their literature repertoire will have been significantly expanded and their comprehension of narrative forms will have taken a quantum leap. And like most mainstream youngsters (those with abundant home and school literacy experiences), they will be very successful with the published materials that are currently used in the early grades. Almost without exception, they will be able to read the stories in their readers as well as handle the extensive worksheets that focus on word analysis skills and that are a part of all published programs. Parents will be pleased, as will teachers and administrators. What will not be understood is that these youngsters will have been engaged in the process of learning to read long before they became first graders and were exposed to published materials. Further, to the extent that the formal reading activities overlook the active engagement with story reading and writing in favor of mechanical analyses of print forms, they short circuit rather than expand these youngsters' literacy development. Three school years of programs in which these youngsters were invited to explore literature and compose their own stories are to be exchanged for a steady diet of truncated narratives about "Dick and Jane" and fill-in-the-blank type worksheets.

It goes without saying that nonmainstream youngsters—those who have not benefited from regular family/school literacy experiences in their preschool years—will not have the same experience when they reach first grade. The formal program typical of most first and second grades is beyond the grasp of these children who have not had an accumulation of pleasurable as well as instructive opportunities to explore books with adults and often signals the beginning of a record of school failure. Typical beginner instructional activities, such as learning that letters stand for speech sounds and putting them in sequences to form words, make sense only to youngsters who have an extensive experience with the end products of written language—namely, books. Put another way, the motivation to learn to read and write comes from having had a long and pleasurable relationship with the world of fiction. As we've seen, understanding stories is a highly specialized task that requires many encounters with books in the company of a reader who can bridge the gap between the child's understanding and the author's message.

Our challenge is to shape literacy programs for the N–K years and the early grades that enhance and extend children's developing relations to written language—whether these are their own creations or those of someone else. And, like the shaping of programs for three-year-olds, these curricula must be open-ended in design so that class groups with a range of experiences with written language will benefit. The remainder of the book outlines key understandings about children, teachers, and literacy education that must guide the shaping of programs for four- through seven-year-olds.

Part III

FOUR– AND FIVE–YEAR–OLDS

7

Coming of Age
Literacy Programs in the N–K Years

Throughout the past 20 years, programs for the nursery–kindergarten ages have proliferated. This has been as much the result of increasing numbers of mothers moving into the work force as of the recognition that early education is useful and helpful. The burgeoning of programs for the young learner, however, has coincided with disenchantment with the academic competence of students at the other end of the educational continuum. Students are graduating from high school and college who do not possess adequate reading and writing skills. Until very recently, scores on widely implemented tests such as the College Board examination have been in steady decline. As the visible evidence of incompetence in reading and writing has grown, parents, teachers, and public officials have focused attention on, first, the high schools, then, the elementary schools, and finally, the kindergarten and nursery classes. While no one believed that early education was to blame for the national decline in academic competence (blame was largely reserved for high schools), it was thought that if youngsters started earlier in educational programs for learning to read, then perhaps we could offset later problems.

During the 1970s, the elementary schools were given the directive to get "back to basics" in their teaching and program design—for example, emphasis was to be placed on the three R's—while preschool programs were, above all, to stress language learning in their curricula. It was during this decade that early education became caught up, as Evelyn Weber (1984) put it, "in the one dominant goal of literacy" (p. 198). The focus on developing early reading programs persists and shows no sign of abating.

CONFLICTING VIEWS OF
LITERACY TEACHING AND LEARNING

How teachers and administrators of young children have responded to the directive to emphasize reading in N–K programs is related to their own be-

How do I think chn unford?

liefs about how children learn to read. Predictably, one of the major responses has been to translate formal methods and materials used in the primary grades into programs for young children. These educators transformed paper and pencil activities that have the skill-drill focus of workbook materials found in the literacy programs for the grades into activities for the kindergarten program. Publishers of reading materials for elementary programs have been quick to provide materials designed to prime young students for their entry into formal reading programs, which begin in the first grade.

Other early childhood teachers have resisted the idea that reading and writing need to be a regular part of N–K programs. When I taught kindergarten, I was one of these teachers. As a group we were often referred to as humanistic teachers, or teachers who believed that the traditional early childhood program with its emphasis on concrete activities was the primary educational experience children needed at this age. We defended our view by saying that these ages were not mature enough to handle the demands of reading and writing—that their abilities to deal with symbols and their hand-eye coordination were not adequately developed. We were, of course, extremely critical of the formal methods and materials associated with the teaching of reading. Such approaches, we loudly proclaimed, did not belong in the kindergarten program.

Along with like-minded colleagues, I was keenly interested in Jean Piaget's investigations of the nature of intellectual development. More than any other thinker of this century, Piaget articulated the child's unique perspective of the world and demonstrated that the development of the sensory-oriented infant to the abstract thinker of preadolescence is systematic and definable. His stage theory of growth describes the general sequence of intellectual growth at the same time that it demonstrates that no two paths of development are identical. These views provide theoretical support for the collaborative method, that is, that to be effective, teachers must attempt to understand the world from the child's perspective.

Those of us who were intrigued by Piaget's views of children's development debated how to implement his ideas in the classroom. While Piaget was prolific in producing descriptions of the nature of children's learning, he was not at all clear about how his ideas might be translated into teaching methods or materials. Nevertheless, we used Piaget's ideas to defend our programs that emphasized hands-on activities and tended to avoid regular and extensive experiences with print. To the degree that reading readiness materials were used, they were mostly representative of what is known as the Language Experience Approach (LEA). Included under this general heading are activities such as labeling items in the classroom, taking children's story dictations, and constructing experience charts about class activities. At every opportunity, we tried to persuade others in the educational world of the wrongness of the effort to begin more formal reading and writing programs in N–K classes.

There was, however, a significant flaw in our case. The facts were that each year some of our five-year-olds could read—indeed, they began their kindergarten year already reading! Parents of these youngsters often pointed out that our programs needed to be expanded in some way to include activities specifically designed for the readers. They were right, and their criticisms simply underscored the indefensibility of our position. It also increased our educational dilemma: how to provide a literacy program for these youngsters that was not modeled on formal reading programs and that was consistent with the collaborative teaching/learning frame outlined by Piaget and other researchers of young children's growth.

As noted in earlier chapters, recent research has confirmed that many of the informal methods used in the home are quite appropriate and legitimate for early childhood classrooms. Ways of transforming these methods for N–K class groups will be discussed in subsequent chapters. Before we move to those descriptions, however, it is useful to examine the informal approach to teaching using the example that follows and to extrapolate general guidelines for designing early childhood programs.

TEACHING/LEARNING PROCESSES IN THE EARLY CHILDHOOD PROGRAM

Three-year-old Christopher and I were standing by the window watching the snow fall in the play yard. It was the first big snow of the winter. Nearly everyone in the class was taking turns looking out of the windows and watching the large flakes slowly cover the yard with a blanket of white. I asked Christopher where he thought the snow came from. After a short pause, he replied, "From that building over there" and pointed to the brick building that backed onto our yard. Surprised by his explanation, I got down next to him so that I was looking out of the window at about the same spot he was. From that perspective, the flakes blended with the sky until they fell in front of the brown bricks. It did, indeed, look as if the flakes were coming out of the building.

I asked Christopher for an explanation, and he provided his hypothesis based on his observations. In common with most children in the three-to-five age range, for Christopher, seeing is believing. Hypothesizing, as noted, is something children do continually as they build their understanding of how the world works. Providing opportunities for children to articulate their ideas-in-progress is part of the teaching task. The real challenge is knowing how to respond to children's hypotheses—especially when they differ from our own more mature or scientific explanations of things. The most typical response is the "yes, but" response: "Yes, it does look as if the snow is coming out of that building, but . . ." (followed by an explanation of why the child's observation is incorrect).

Piaget (1973) states that to deny the child's view by substituting the correct explanation is to intrude upon children's learning.

> In order to understand certain basic phenomena through the combination of deductive reasoning and the data of experience, the child must pass through a certain number of stages characterized by ideas which will later be judged erroneous but which appear necessary in order to reach the final correct solution. (p. 21)

In Piaget's terms, the child's ability to reason from experience represents the heart of the learning process. It is this process that is responsible for the experimental mind and that, more than any other, sets the stage for a lifetime of learning. To intrude upon this process by providing explanations that the child has neither the experience nor the mental maturity to grasp is to distort a teaching/learning moment. In the case of Christopher and the snow, the first part of the teaching response (the one I used) was to confirm his observation: "Yes, it does look as if the snow is coming from the building." Such a response is typical of many early childhood teachers; it tends to characterize the humanistic, as opposed to the teaching-as-telling, approach. Teachers of N–K classes accept the fact that children don't "see" things the same way as adults do. Nor do the teachers require that youngsters' views be immediately revised to conform to a more mature understanding. However, if the "yes, but" teachers have erred on the side of saying too much, humanists have tended to err on the side of saying too little. As I did with Christopher, we tend to end the exchange with our confirmation of the child's views rather than use this information to think through an appropriate follow-up action.

What has been overlooked is that not only do youngsters need opportunities to reason from experience, but they also need chances to expand the knowledge base from which they derive their understanding of how things work. This is the next part of the teaching/learning event. One way to help Christopher to re-evaluate his hypothesis would be to expand his experience by providing, for example, another angle for viewing the falling snow: "Yes, it does look as if the snow is coming from the building. Let's go over to the other window and see what it looks like from there." Presumably, from that angle the snow won't look as if it is coming from the building. Experiences that conflict with Christopher's current ideas about snow will, in time, prompt him to revise his hypothesis. It is this kind of friction—"cognitive disequilibrium" in Piaget's terms—that stimulates children, or adults, for that matter, to rethink their theories about how things work.

In general, informal or collaborative interactions are sequenced as follows:

1. Teachers (or children) raise questions
2. Teachers ask for and/or appreciate the child's reasoning and/or hypotheses
3. Teachers use the child's current views to guide them in the design of subsequent teaching/learning experiences

This sequence replicates the handover principle described in the beginning chapters as the major strategy through which adults guide children's learning. Put briefly, the idea is to provide experiences that children can learn from rather than explanations that they are asked to repeat or imitate.

This teaching/learning sequence not only is appropriate for learning about the physical world but it applies to symbolic learning as well. Nursery and kindergarten teachers need to take note that this process can be effectively used to shape literacy programs that are consistent with humanistic, child-centered approaches to teaching. To me, it is painfully ironic that those of us who were the more "traditional" early childhood educators were the most resistant to the idea that literacy programs had a rightful place in the N–K programs. The dilemma that we faced has been well described by Harste, Burke, and Woodward (1984), as follows:

> The assumption that one must begin literacy learning with letter and sound matching is so pervasive that many otherwise excellent early childhood educators are not interested in highlighting reading and writing activities in the pre-school. . . . With "new" materials advocating a skills and drills approach to beginning reading and writing, their observations of the written language concepts "Sesame Street" teaches, and their past experience with formal literacy programs, these teachers believe that to stress literacy they must abandon their humanistic learning model. *By not being aware of either their assumptions or theoretical alternatives, they permit their children to miss many significant and natural encounters with print.* (p. 62, emphasis added)

Because we avoided the use of the formal published materials, there tended to be a vacuum in our literacy programs for four- and five-year-olds. That learning to read and write should derive from youngsters' interests and initiatives was the way we knew it should be done. What was lacking was a clear understanding of the developmental course of reading and writing and an appreciation of the significance of children's early efforts in this area. With these aspects of literacy development more clearly defined, we have the unique opportunity to create early childhood programs in which literacy programs reflect informal teaching approaches.

The theoretical alternatives referred to in the above quotation represent the general teaching/learning approaches to be explored in the following two chapters. The understanding that there is continuity between learning in and out of school and between learning about the physical world and the symbolic world must guide the design of literacy programs for N–K classes.

8

Children's Writing Repertoire

Two months after Kimberly produced her rhyme story "Shama sheema
. . ." (see Chapter 5), I heard her singing/chanting a verse with the distinct
rhythms of a popular song. I got my pad and pen and asked her to repeat it
a little louder so I could write it down. Eyeing my pen and pad, she said she
would write it down. I said I wasn't sure I could read her writing—so could
she say it so I could write it and then she could write it her way? What I
recorded was apparently her version of a rock song:

Yes man, you say/ N' you wanna say
You wanna say/ And run around
Yes man, you wanna say/ And o.k. . . .
Jumpety jumpety jumpety jump/ And yuppy sup.

When Kimberly stopped singing, she took my pad and pen in hand and
began to write her verse (see Figure 8.1). Her writing is interesting because
it reveals her view of written language. Indeed, her approximation of words-
written-down has the "look" of manuscript: Letter-like shapes are repeated
and arranged linearly. This graphic representation was quite unlike her drawings and indicated that she understood that there is a difference between
drawing and writing. At this point in the year, many in my class of three's
turning four were exploring writing forms along with their drawing.

Similar to Christopher's hypothesis about where snow comes from Kimberly is learning about the world of symbols through experimenting and hypothesizing about principles that govern the converting of speech to print.
Because children's writing approximations never resemble standard writing
samples, adults tend to respond skeptically to the child's request for support
and approval of these creations as real writing. We smile and comment on
how cute the sample is. We do not interpret these efforts as the time to welcome children into the community of writers, as we welcome them into the
community of talkers when they produce their first approximations of

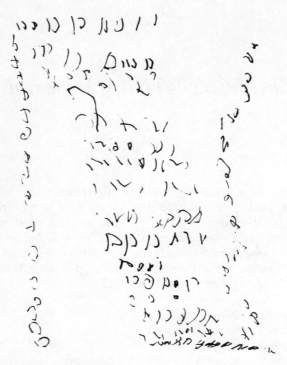

Figure 8.1 *Kimberly writes her song*   (Source: Gibson-Geller, 1985, p.23)

speech. Similar to our attitude toward children's early reading, we believe these efforts have very little connection to real writing.

Typical of beginner writers, Kimberly has separated transcription from composition. These two aspects of written language—composing (the content) and transcription (the form)—tend to evolve as separate threads in the growth of children's writing abilities. With young children, composing tends to develop well in advance of the ability to transcribe. Many three-year-olds, we've noted, have grasped key elements of storytelling. Often they have begun to use book language and to include common plot features in their dictated compositions. For most youngsters it takes many years of exploration and practice before composing and transcribing, the warp and woof of writing, become integrated so that one translates almost immediately into the other. For many youngsters in N–K classes, these pieces of the writing pie have begun to come together, and spontaneously generated letters/words/phrases begin to appear embedded in their drawings. During these early school years, youngsters are willing and eager, given proper encouragement, to explore their developing hypotheses regarding the transcription system of spoken language. During the years from two through eight, youngsters experiment simultaneously with print forms of three general types: writing approximations, print practice, and alphabetic writing. These categories form the core of young children's writing repertoire.

WRITING APPROXIMATIONS

Many youngsters begin to experiment with writing long before the N–K years. A typical example of this kind of exploration is that of two-year-old Adam. He picked up the ballpoint pen next to the pad of paper on the telephone table. Slowly and carefully he made one shape after another on the pad (see Figure 8.2). When asked what he was doing, he responded, "Makin ledders." Having learned, apparently, that the forms that constitute print are called "letters," he was motivated to produce his version of these shapes. For the toddler who is just beginning to separate drawing and writing, the print approximations derive from his or her visual images of what writing looks like. In contrast to his writing, when asked to draw, Adam enjoyed covering the paper with quickly executed, linear forms. The important point is not which marks were made for which activity—some children use linear shapes for writing and circular shapes for drawing—but rather the fact that Adam made such a distinction. That reveals that he has begun to categorize differences between these modes of two-dimensional expression. This kind of defining and separating of shapes and forms represents the route by which Adam will, over the next four to six years, master most writing conventions.

Four-year-old Sandy was patiently standing in line with her mother, who was waiting to register for two graduate courses in education. The line was moving very slowly, and Sandy was becoming increasingly restless. Her mother gave her a blank registration form and a ballpoint pen. Sandy knelt on the floor and filled in each of the empty blanks on the form with linear expansions that were her versions of cursive writing. She was careful not to go outside of the guidelines, and, from a distance, her form looked very much like her mother's. Sandy's mother explained to me that filling out forms was currently a favorite activity. Sandy was especially eager to take trips to the bank because she had discovered that when she pressed very hard on the top page of a deposit slip, the mark came through to the page underneath.

Five-year-old Joshua was sitting at the typewriter in the writing center of his classroom. Having just figured out how to position the paper, he was busy pushing the keys and watching the results line up on the page. After he had produced five lines of letters, numbers, and other shapes represented on the keyboard, he pulled the paper out and took it to his teacher (see Figure

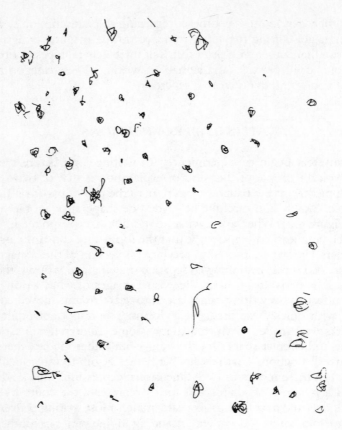

Figure 8.2   Adam: "Makin ledders"

8.3). "Look at my book!" he said proudly. Youngsters like Joshua, who already know something about the names and shapes of letters and who even write their names as well as other words, are prompted to use writing approximations when tackling what is for them a new and complex project. In a brief exchange with his teacher, Joshua revealed that he was aware that a "real" book was made up of "somebody's words" and that he had just put letters and shapes together so that they "kind of looked like words in a book." Unlike Adam, who believed that his letters were authentic, Joshua knew that his book was a pretend version of the real thing. He was intrigued with the visual likeness to lines of print in a book, which he could achieve on a typewriter.

Nearly all children experiment with writing by reproducing print forms

THU&YOUUO$4veur6yy6yyruwnLJ7647uJh5Lyy4677rhGc ygufhry yLLyur7767GgLLdggdL
ayyfyyyHRYYU¢YYO%¢T%¦"?IKMYhyrG656-hu___JCTCBCBCOGTVDRH-ghiR&ll¢TO&¢¢YRTY$&Y$¢¢YR
OOYTHHMTTah uruy74uO9O777y7&¢$¢%¢¢T266Gt'}...//.. ,,rhyygg//?NJOYTRTOR$TTTRTD%B
YYRY¢THHVNVNVHHYYUYYY&¢YOTOO3YYYYYU1OO17G6urG7OOuuy   TKEEOFlX HYHHCHNNCHHCHCNCNC
UFY¢¢Y%&¦;/rG55fh7¢¢GTTTE%YOOOAAB OU**Y***HCG¢¢¢N ?CNNUUYH&HHYKKJJJHN'tJnyhfhhhJ
hfy6ryuy hhOGYYOHYYH NVNUHODDDJOU

Figure 8.3   *Joshua: "Look at my book!"*

that have the "look" of text. Sometimes they focus on the generalized shapes
of discrete letters. At other times they are mindful of the spatial organization
of a page of print, that is, that it proceeds in lines and fills up most of the
space.

PRINT PRACTICE

Writing One's Own Name

David, just turned four and the oldest boy in the class, responded to his
teacher's request to write his name by picking up the orange crayon she had
placed next to a sheet of white paper and carefully forming a *D* in the upper
left-hand corner (see Figure 8.4). He surveyed what he had done, said that
the *D* "wasn't right," and produced another one. Then he made the *A, V*
(upside down), an *i*, and the final *D,* moving from left to right across the top
of the page. When he had finished, he quickly moved away from the table to
the block building area. He seemed eager to explore materials that, for him,
did not require the same precision as printing his name.

David revealed his understanding of many writing conventions in this

Figure 8.4   *David writes his name*

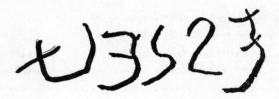

Figure 8.5 *Jesse writes his name*

sample. He has learned which letters make up his name and he has a mental image—especially in relation to the *D*—of how each should be shaped. Further, he knows that the letters need to be placed in a certain sequence and that they need to be written from left to right.

When five-year-old Jesse was asked to write his name, he spoke of the difficulties he has with this task (see Figure 8.5). After producing a *U* shape, he looked at it carefully and then wrote the horizontal line on the left side. It was at this point that he warned his teacher, "Sometimes, I get it wrong." He proceeded with the *E,* the first *S,* and then the second *S.* He stopped and looked at the two *S*'s together and said, "That one [the second one] looks like a 2." Then he wrote the final *E.*

Mastering the writing of one's own name is a "trailblazing event," say Temple, Nathan, and Burris in their book *The Beginnings of Writing* (1982, p. 47). They point out that this accomplishment provides youngsters with much information about the writing system. Watching adults write their names as well as producing their own versions teaches children about sequencing and directionality.

The pleasure children experience in writing their names continues to grow as they move into the early grades. Primary-age children who are experienced and fluent writers of their names frequently use this special bit of writing as the medium for their first attempt at cursive writing. Their confidence in their ability to write their names provides a sense of security when they enter this uncharted territory. Also, the ubiquitous labels which fill every classroom—usually produced by the teacher in N–K groups—can be created by primary-age youngsters who relish the chance to transform the letters of their names into colorful and artistic graphic designs.

Letter Shapes

As children expand their opportunities for practicing print, they become increasingly aware of the contours that differentiate one letter from another. "I know how to make a *Y,*" said four-year-old Alex to the group sitting around the drawing/writing table. He picked up a pencil and one of the little

Figure 8.6   *Alex: "I know how to make a 'Y'"*

pads of paper on the table and began by making a *V*. "See, first you make a *V* and then you put a tail on it" (see Figure 8.6).

Sydney, who was sitting next to Alex, was working on a note to the director of the school. "Dear Marion,' she dictated to her teacher, "I like to be in dress-up." She signed her name at the bottom of the note, folded it, and put it in one of the envelopes the teacher provided for letter writing. Sydney started to write her name on the front of the envelope, and her teacher explained that this was the place where you write the name of the person to whom you are sending the letter. The teacher took a strip of paper and wrote "To Marion" on it and placed it in front of Sydney. With much careful scrutiny of each letter, Sydney copied the phrase (see Figure 8.7). "*M*'s," she noted out loud, "are like *N*'s—they just have an extra line at the end." Her *a* was a circle with a "tail." She transformed the lowercase *r* in the model to an uppercase *R*: a circle with two diagonal lines attached to the bottom. Then she produced the *i* with the *o* attached to it, and the final *n*. As she checked her version with the model, she felt that the "look" of the attached *i* and *o* was inappropriate so she inserted another *i*.

Temple, Nathan, and Burris (1982) point out that there is a lapse of

Figure 8.7   *Sydney addresses her note to Marion*

months or years between the time children begin to experiment with letters and the time they master the 26 letter shapes of our alphabet:

> During that time, they may be constantly surprised that letters they know can be varied to produce new letters. For example, the letter *d* may be turned upside down to make a letter *p*, or flipped around to make a letter *b*. If we add two horizontal bars to the letter, *L*, we get *E*; if we take the lower bar off *E*, we get *F*. (p. 35)

Mastering letter shapes cannot be accomplished simply by imitation or memorization. If this were the case, then the young learner would have to memorize literally hundreds of shapes. The form of a particular letter comprises a family of shapes. Any one form can be written in many different ways depending upon the manuscript system of a particular keyboard or the idiosyncracies of personal penmanship. Rather than a memorization task, mastering the 52 letter shapes (26 uppercase and 26 lowercase) is mostly a matter of developing a mental image that underscores the essence of the letter shape at the same time that it allows for variability in representation. The task requires active efforts to abstract and generalize letter forms so that the essences are separated from the idiosyncracies. In order to derive the needed generalizations, children need ample opportunities to compare one shape with another—abstracting the similarities and differences—as they build a separate mental category for each of the letter forms.

The fine discriminations that children need to make in mastering letter shapes can take place only when children are provided with many opportunities to practice writing: Tracing, copying, and generating one's own letters and words all need to be a part of the N–K program. Further, watching others write (older peers, parents, and teachers) needs to be a regular part of the teaching/learning process. In this way the dynamic and functional principles of writing are continually demonstrated:

> If writing proceeds from left to right, then children must see someone doing it to comprehend this point. If writing can record a message and convey it to a distant receiver, then children must participate in the family [or school] drama of remembering absent friends, thinking of a message for them, writing the messages down, sealing them up, and mailing them out. (Temple, Nathan, & Burris, 1982, p. 52)

A point to be stressed is that forms and functions of writing need to be integrated as often as possible so that children learn to write by writing for purposes that they understand and that they have had a part in planning.

Most of the published materials designed for N–K classrooms are workbook type activities. Letters are studied in isolation. A page of *d*'s, for example, is followed by a page of another letter. This tends to obscure rather than contribute to possibilities for comparison, which are necessary, as noted, to comprehend the essence of a single letter form. Youngsters who may be experiencing their first opportunities to explore letter shapes need to begin with a small group of letters, preferably those of their names, so that they can compare one shape with another. On the other hand, for children who come to school with relatively stable concepts of many of the letter shapes, worksheets represent little more than busy work. These more able youngsters are better off generating their own writing. Worksheets, by definition, separate letter learning from its function or purpose. This reverses the process by which children learn about writing outside of school. In that process, form follows function, such as in home settings where children observe family members writing to take care of family needs. Indeed, probably the best way to describe the shortcomings of worksheets is that, for those who can do them, they contribute little to their learning; and for those who can't, they do not provide the kind of opportunities needed to expand the children's understanding of print functions and forms. As a result, for both groups of children, worksheets tend to represent a waste of their language learning time.

Exploring Patterns

Five-year-old April was practicing writing by constructing lines of single letters (left to right/top to bottom) (see Figure 8.8). When asked what she had written, she answered, "Words." From her answer we can surmise that one of her current hypotheses regarding relations between spoken and written language is that strings of letters represent words. What she still has to come to terms with is the notion that these "strings" need to be in a specific order (Genishi & Dyson, 1984, p. 173).

Children also experiment with sentence frames and patterns, and often discover that if they know how to write the first few words of the sentence, they can generate a lot of text by simply changing the final word or object in the same sentence frame (Clay, 1975, p. 57) (see Figure 8.9). Children appear to be pleased both with the possibility of filling up an entire page with print and with organizing the writing pattern in such a way that each word (or letter) is written separately. In Figure 8.9, for example, the *I*'s and the lowercase *l*'s seem to have been written in vertical lines before the child moved on to the next part of the sentence.

This impulse to look for print patterns and to reproduce words or phrases by repeating discrete items continues into the early grades, when homework assignments often require repeated writings of, say, the multiplication tables and spelling words. Youngsters line up the equations or words and produce vertical lines of the same letter or number. Though this is an efficient method

Figure 8.8 *April's words*   (Source: Genishi & Dyson, 1984, p.173)

for taking care of the assignments, it obscures and even distorts the principles that describe multiplication and spelling processes. In lieu of an active analysis of number or spelling features, youngsters become engaged in attempts to master the material by rote. And as any student, old or young, can confirm, this kind of learning lasts only long enough "to get through the test." What we need to remember, then, is that youngsters are willing to spend a great deal of time practicing print (or number) patterns for purposes that they have designed for themselves. When, however, teachers do the structuring of tasks built upon repetition, the boredom of the task invites youngsters to find a way to get the job done quickly, rather than to think about what they are doing.

ALPHABETIC WRITING: LEARNING TO SPELL

English orthography, or spelling system, is a complicated, albeit logical, system of rules and principles for converting speech to print. First and foremost

Figure 8.9 *Experimenting with sentence patterns* (Source: Clay, 1975, p.57)

it is based on the alphabetic principle. This means that it is phonemes, or the separate sounds within words, that are represented by print symbols. For example, my first name, Linda, has five separate phonemes and is written with five letters.

But we don't always have a one-to-one correspondence between speech sounds and letters. Because there are more sounds (about 44) than letters (26) to represent them, many letters must stand for more than one sound. The most common examples are the vowels—one letter for both long and short pronunciations. Also, there are many consonants (*c, s, g, z, x*), as well as blends and digraphs, in which letters do double duty in representing two or more phonemes. To further complicate things, a single sound can be represented by many different letters or spellings. The long *e*, for example, can be represented by 13 different spellings. This is a surprising statistic, of which few people who are not language specialists are aware.

Alphabetic writing is a highly economic form of notation. Through combining and recombining the 26 letters of our alphabet to represent more than 40 sounds of our spoken language, we can spell and write the thousands of words that make up the English lexicon. The nature of this system is underscored when compared with logographic writing, the transcription system for the Chinese language. Here each word is represented by a different symbol. As a result, a literate person in the Chinese culture must learn thousands of symbols, called characters, in order to read and write the language.

When learning to spell, English-speaking children begin with their approximations of sound-to-print rules and, with regular practice, slowly master the extensive rule system that defines English orthography. And just as we accept and celebrate the infant/toddler's first approximations in speech and reading, so we must accept and appreciate youngsters' early spelling efforts.

Early Phonemic Spelling

According to her mother, Giti first provided evidence of experimentation with the alphabetic system by associating the /g/ sound and letter *G* of her name with the names of her grandparents. At 26 months, writes Baghban (1984), "she practiced *G*s and in [certain instances] labeled them Giti, Grandma, and Grandpa, perceiving that each name began with the same sound and letters" (p. 56).

This use of a single consonant to represent a word can be found in the samples of many youngsters' early writing. This makes sense because generally consonant sounds begin words and are stressed more than vowel sounds. The following example of early phonemic spelling was produced by a five-year-old (Temple, Nathan, & Burris, 1982, p. 81):

MiBEhoTOSL (My baby home to sleep.)

In this example, the youngster has attempted to go beyond a phonemic representation of the first letter of a word and has produced another letter, most often the second one, in each of the words. This example highlights three aspects of the written code with which children must struggle as they build their understanding of the alphabetic principle:

1. What level of a word sound does a phoneme represent?
2. Which letters represent which sounds?
3. What is a word?

In the example above, the kindergartener has begun to segment a word into phonemes and to match these sounds with the letters that represent them (1 and 2 above). What is still not understood is the concept of *word*. Spoken language, it must be remembered, proceeds without breaks between one word and another. The understanding that speech comprises discrete words rather than strings of uninterrupted sounds is a large step. Many opportunities to observe adults write as well as shared reading experiences provide needed exposure to this critical feature of written language.

Letter-Name Spelling

While the early phonemic writer provides evidence of a rudimentary understanding of sound-to-print correspondences, as youngsters move along in their experiments with spelling, they begin to refine their abilities to make sound-to-letter correspondences. Figure 8.10 is a good example of how the letter-name strategy for spelling works. Amy, a kindergartener, wrote a note

Figure 8.10   *Amy's note to Linda*

to a favorite student teacher (Linda) who had recently been transferred to another classroom. The note, with translation, reads: Dr (Dear) LND (Linda) I(I) LV (love) U (you) Km (come) VST (visit) mE (me).

Amy has segmented both beginning and ending sounds of words. None of the short vowels have been represented. This is not surprising, because these phonemes tend to be the most difficult to discriminate. Long vowel sounds, however, do appear (*i*, *u*, and *e* in *me*). In this case, the letters *I* and the *U* are used to represent words. The logic by which Amy has arrived at these invented spellings is to use the name of the letter as the clue for deciding which letter should represent which sound/word, that is, *dee* has the /d/ sound within it. The same is true of the names for most of the consonants and long vowels. Consistent with this strategy for representing sounds, the *c* in *come* is represented by the letter *k*. Letter-name spellers tend to represent the *s* in *visit* with an *s*, as Amy has done, or with a *z* (depending upon how you pronounce *visit*, the middle consonant can be sounded with the emphasis on the "hiss" or the "buzz").

For youngsters like Amy, learning the names of the letters of the alphabet provides a logical basis for representing speech. What is interesting to note is that, unlike early phonemic writing, most adults are able to decode Amy's message, given the context of her note to Linda. The point is that when youngsters begin to use the alphabetic principle as a main spelling strategy, they have taken a large step toward mastering the English written language system.

Another example of letter-name writing is from a five-year-old boy (Temple, Nathan, & Burris, 1982, p. 78):

A MAN ROB SOS THE PLES FID HEM (A man robbed shoes. The police found him.)

The discrete spacing of each word indicates that this youngster has a better idea of what a word is than Amy does. Further, the spelling of some of the words in his writing repertoire has been memorized (*man, the, a*). Words for which he invents the spelling have been segmented into their phonemic elements, and the letter-name strategy has been used to represent these sounds. For example, in the spelling HEM (*him*), the *e* is chosen to represent the *i* because of the articulation similarities. When you repeat the word slowly, the short /i/ sound in this word is voiced in the back of the throat as is the beginning sound of the name for the letter *e*. In the early stages of letter-name spelling, articulation patterns represent a major strategy for representing short vowel sounds, the most difficult sounds, as noted, to separate from the rest of the word (Read, 1975).

Youngsters who indicate that they have grasped these basic aspects of the alphabetic code face yet other challenges as they move along in their understanding of spelling principles. Languages that use the alphabetic system for their written versions vary in complexity as a result of the rules that govern sound-to-letter combinations. For those languages that are phonetically regular—that is, in which there is nearly a one-to-one correspondence between each spoken sound and its written representation—the learning-to-spell process tends to be relatively simple. Once youngsters learn the letters of the alphabet and the sound each represents, they have pretty much mastered the spelling system. Spanish and Italian are good examples of languages whose written versions are represented by this kind of consistency between sound and symbol. Many native speakers of these languages have commented that they remember the relative ease with which they learned to spell and write. This contrasts sharply with the memories of many of us who are native English speakers and writers. Transitional spelling represents the final phase of coming to terms with English orthography and is more typical of the spelling difficulties of primary-age children (see Chapter 11) than of N–K children.

GUIDELINES FOR TEACHERS OF N–K CLASSES

The challenge to teachers currently working with young children is to make sure that appropriate spelling and writing programs are put in place right from the beginning. For the N–K years, this means that teachers must be very familiar with the general sequence of growth as well as typical spelling-writing inventions that characterize children's early writing. Further, it needs to be understood that growth in this area cannot be described as a simple march from an exploration of nonstandard spelling to the application of standard transcription rules. Rather, children's development tends to move, simultaneously, in horizontal as well as vertical directions. The horizontal movement is represented by children's concurrent explorations of writing approximations, print patterns, and alphabetic writing. As noted, they move among these three general categories of writing during the period of intense investigation and experimentation with systems of transcription that characterize the N–K and primary years. At the same time, however, vertical growth is underway as youngsters move from less mature to more mature methods for transcribing language. Sulzby and Teale (1985) describe the process as follows:

> The same child may use scribble for one story, letter strings for another, write his name conventionally, and write a list of words in a mix of conventional and invented spellings. Although it may be possible to observe an overall pattern of development from less sophisticated to more sophisticated writing strategies and knowledge, the process of development as it occurs within individual children, is much more complicated. (p. 10)

Teachers' appreciation of the horizontal and vertical directions of writing development go hand in hand with providing contexts for writing. The general goal is to find useful and appropriate ways for expanding the child's knowledge of transcription strategies, that is, to provide meaningful situations in which children write and observe people writing. To repeat what has been said before, hypothesis formation and revision represents the heart of language learning processes; it is the primary method through which children construct their understanding of both the spoken and written language systems. Such a perspective of language learning translates into the following goals for N–K writing and spelling programs:

1. To confirm the youngster's beginning, or incomplete, perspectives of the spelling system
2. To expand the child's awareness by adding more related information
3. To provide opportunities for the child to engage in the exploration of his or her current spelling methods

In N–K class groups, teachers are likely to have youngsters with a wide range of abilities, and, as a result, the range of the spelling-writing behaviors described are likely to be represented in a single class. As examples of differing strategies appear, teachers need to confirm or describe to the child his or her approach: "John, I see you like to make patterns out of the words and phrases that you are writing." Next, the teacher must be deliberate in sharing one child's approach with others: "Look, everyone, John has arranged his writing this way. How is this the same as (different from) the way (someone else) has done it?" In this way, the teacher heightens the children's awareness of the range of approaches to transcribing words and phrases.

The teacher must also write or record in front of the children words, phrases, and sentences that have personal meaning for individuals or for the class group. At these times, teachers need to underscore print conventions by describing what they are doing. Discussions of letter shapes and letter-sound relations, and awareness of what a word is need to be integrated into teachers' and children's daily writing functions and creations. As examples are highlighted and displayed, a class spelling-writing repertoire will begin to take shape. Finally, teachers need to provide regular time and materials for youngsters to practice writing. In this way, youngsters will slowly expand their writing repertoire to include more approaches and refine their grasp of alphabetic, visual, and semantic strategies that govern transcription rules.

9

Teaching Reading in Kindergarten

One way to think about the task of teaching reading to beginners is to compare the learning process with that experienced by a mature reader when confronted with unfamiliar material. For example, my knowledge and understanding of the law is limited at best. Legal contracts and briefs represent text types with which I have had little experience. When approaching such material, I bring many of the characteristics associated with an immature reader. I read slowly, word by word, and reread sections frequently. When I identify a word that I sense is critical to my understanding of the text, I refer to a dictionary, which may or may not be helpful because I am unfamiliar with the legal connotations of meanings associated with these words and phrases. Mostly, I search for the essence of the message—what do I have to do, when, and how.

Depending upon the extent of my difficulties with the text and the seriousness of the issue, I may need to go over the material with my lawyer. He functions as a mediator between me and the text, much the same way as parents and teachers of young children do during storytimes. As we progress through the text, I raise questions and request explanations. My lawyer, of course, has developed a fluency with this material which I will never have. Indeed, it is unlikely that I will ever achieve the kind of independence in reading and interpreting material of this type that I have achieved with, say, literature or education texts.

The point is that once transcription patterns are mastered, reading competence is determined by the degree of familiarity a reader has with the particular linguistic and conceptual structures that define a subject. If I were to attempt mastery of legal language and thinking, I would need to be very deliberate in following a course of study that would bring me in contact with experienced thinkers in this area who could guide me through encounters with legal concepts and texts. In short, I would need to go to law school. Regular discussions of legal ideas would be necessary to familiarize me with basic tenets of this conceptual system. Beginning reading experiences would include reading and discussing relatively uncomplicated material. With increasing experience, I would be able to expand the variety and complexity of the material that I would be capable of handling, first with a guide and subsequently on my own.

Young children need a similarly structured program to introduce them to written language. In the school setting, reading programs must include regular opportunities for children to interact with a variety of texts in a variety of ways. Three types of experiences with written language need to be provided as a part of the daily reading program:

1. *Conceptual preparation:* Reading aloud by the teacher of old and new material, with ample time for discussing the meanings of what is read
2. *Guided reading:* Opportunities for a teacher-directed investigation of text content (meanings) and form (transcription rules)
3. *Independent reading:* Opportunities to explore and read text materials individually

Together these constitute a teaching approach built upon the understanding of the process of learning to read as one in which the youngsters must be, first and foremost, active investigators and processors of text materials. In terms of an educational model, this approach represents an extension of the informal literacy learning experiences many children are exposed to in their homes and nursery classrooms. The teaching/learning process is based on the handover principle. As described earlier, in these kinds of interactions the emphasis is on children learning from, rather than imitating, adult demonstrations of reading behaviors. How these teaching methods can be translated into practice in a kindergarten classroom is described below. The examples are taken from an all-day kindergarten in a public school in New York City.

CONCEPTUAL PREPARATION: READING ALOUD

The first time I walked into Diane Epstein's classroom, I felt as if I had stepped into a world created for (and by) young children. The walls were decorated with children's work—their stories about life in and out of school—as well as enlarged renditions of favorite examples of children's stories and rhymes. Sam, the pet rabbit, hopped around the room, nosing his way into everything and everyone close to floor level. There was a hamster cage in one corner and a terrarium for a turtle in another. Art materials and a puppet stage were very prominent and very much in use at that moment.

I arrived during the language arts work time, the period of the day when the children explore language-related activities independently. The children were grouped according to their assigned tasks. A steady hum of talking, at times vigorous and excited, could be heard in all areas of the room. Diane and my student advisee circulated around the room encouraging youngsters, making suggestions, or simply appreciating what each one was doing.

Diane's language learning program differed in one important respect from most other kindergarten programs, and that was its design. Not only was there greater emphasis on reading activities, but, more significantly, the teaching approach was consistent with how young children learn. Neither an informal rendition of a formal program, nor an expanded version of a language experience approach (although aspects of that approach were included), Diane's program had a particular shape and design that were based to a large extent on the design of programs for the infant schools (those for five- to seven-year-olds) in New Zealand (Holdaway, 1979, 1984). It was a lively and pleasurable program, perfectly matched to her youngsters' varied experiences with written language.

One of the things my students who worked with Diane noted, with some surprise, was how much reading aloud she did with the group—not just at a regular storytime, which usually ended the morning, but also at other moments during the day. A main motivation for storytimes, Diane explained, was to extend children's knowledge of the world through books. Throughout the year, themes related to children's interests formed the content of many program activities. Those related to life experiences included exploring their families and their neighborhood. Fall and spring seasons inspired investigations of planting, harvesting, cooking, and eating. Also, Diane is aware, as many kindergarten teachers are, that five-year-olds are fascinated by dinosaurs. Thus she frequently organizes class explorations of the habits, types, and sizes of these leviathans from a past epoch.

In these thematic explorations, books formed a central source for finding information. Illustrations as well as texts provided information about many social and physical aspects of life in the present or past. Books that had been shared with the group were prominently displayed and frequently referred to as more and different questions evolved out of class projects and discussions.

Additionally, throughout the year, reading aloud was a time when the group explored the world of literature. Like Louise, with her three-year-olds, Diane's purpose was to continue to expand the literature repertoire of her youngsters through story reading and discussions. Becoming a mature reader is, by definition, a process in which the range and complexity of text structures that a reader can grasp steadily increase. During the years from five to seven, children begin to identify common characteristics of story forms. The fairy tale, the cumulative plot, and the problem story represent some of the story forms with which children must become familiar. As noted, it is the grasp of story structure that makes unfamiliar material more predictable and helps beginners to approach new texts.

The adult's job as mediator between students and text types and styles begins with the first family storybook sessions and should continue as long as there are new forms to be explored. What is interesting is that when we begin to teach reading, we tend to stop reading aloud to youngsters. We come back to it only in high school and college English classes when, because the focus is on raising students' literary awareness, it is thought that an appreciation of genre and style is best taught through hearing and discussing text excerpts. What needs to be understood is that literary awareness is probably the most important contributor not only to the continuing growth of an experienced reader, but also to the reading development of the beginner. If young children understand the ideas and concepts that shape the meaning of a book, then the job of deciphering print details, a major task for the beginner, becomes much easier.

GUIDED READING: THE SHARED–BOOK EXPERIENCE

On another morning, I visited the class during the first period of the day so that I could observe (and audiotape) the guided-reading session led by Donna Lavery, one of my students. Diane encouraged her student teachers to design and lead shared-reading sessions based on her clear and well-defined model. The class gathered on the rug in the library corner. The group faced a poster-sized pad that had a story on it and rested on an easel, making it high enough so that everyone could see it. The text had been copied from *Hello,* a story from the collection, *The Story Box in the Classroom* (Butler, 1984), designed especially for shared reading. A transcript of the beginning of the session follows, with the book text shown in italics:

CHILDREN (Reading in unison): Hello

A donkey says to a donkey,/ Hee haw, hee haw, hee haw.
A lion says to a lion,/ Roar, roar, roar.
A dog says to a dog/ Bow wow wow.
A cat says to a cat/ Meow, meow, meow.
A turkey says to a turkey,/ Gobble, gobble, gobble.
A fish says to a fish/ Bubble, bubble, bubble.
I say to the people I know,/ Hello, hello, hello.

CHILD: Let's read that again.
CHILDREN: Nooooo . . . Yes . . . Yeeeesss . . . yes, yes, yes.
TEACHER: I can't read anything 'til everyone is quiet.
CHILDREN: Read the story again. . . .

The shared-book experience is designed to replicate and extend the story-time experience of the family. In this class, *Hello* has been read many times at other guided-reading sessions, and its meanings have been thoroughly explored and enjoyed prior to the introduction of reading in unison. In terms of text types, it belongs in the predictable book category. Like *Old Mac-Donald Had a Farm,* which was a favorite selection for shared reading with two-year-old Giti and her mother, this text is easily committed to memory. As noted earlier, beginning readers need help entering into the world of print, and this kind of patterned text provides predictability through its simple story line and repeated and rhythmical phrases.

The class was very accomplished at reading in unison. They waited until Donna gave a signal to begin. She indicated the pace by using a ruler to point to each word as they read. This was not a reading in which only a few children's voices could be heard along with the adult leading the way. Their rendition of *Hello* had the vigor and delight usually associated with children's repetitions of game chants and rhymes on the playground.

The shared-book experience, a phrase coined by writers and researchers in New Zealand (Holdaway 1979), has come to represent the heart of the literacy program in early childhood classrooms like Diane's. For the beginner reader, the choral reading of predictable and delightful texts reproduced in large print bridges the gap between story listening and story reading.

The session continued with Donna putting one of the big books on the easel. *Mrs. Wishy-washy,* also from *The Story Box in the Classroom* (Butler, 1984), was another favorite selection of this group. A chorus of "Yeaas" and "Yeses" greeted the appearance of the book. Like the first story, the group has heard and read this one many times. And as they did in reading *Hello,* they began this story together and read straight through, full voiced and with palpable enthusiasm. The text is reproduced below.

Mrs. Wishy-washy. (cover)
Mrs. Wishy-washy. (title)
"Oh, lovely mud," said the cow, and she jumped in it. (pp. 2,3)
"Oh, lovely mud," said the pig, and he rolled in it. (pp. 4,5)
"Oh, lovely mud," said the duck, and she paddled in it. (pp. 6,7)
Along came Mrs. Wishy-washy. "Just LOOK at you!" she screamed. (pp. 8,9)
"In the tub you go." In went the cow, wishy-washy, wishy-washy. (pp. 10,11)

In went the pig, wishy-washy, wishy-washy. (p. 12)
In went the duck, wishy-washy, wishy-washy. (p. 13)
"THAT'S better," said Mrs. Wishy-washy, and she went into the house. (p. 14)
Away went the cow. Away went the pig. Away went the duck. (p. 15)
"OH LOVELY MUD," they said. (p. 16; The final illustration shows the three mud lovers once again thoroughly immersed in the mud puddle.)

Print Conventions

As the reading ended, Donna pointed to the enlarged print on the final page and asked why everyone read that line so loud? One child responded: "Cause the words look louder . . . look bigger . . . and it looks like they're really screaming. . . ." Donna turned back to page 9, where Mrs. Wishy-washy's line (Just LOOK at you!) was given special rendering. The children repeated the line, and one youngster added that the "upside down *i*" was also an indication that the passage should be read "really loud." Donna asked for the name of that punctuation mark, and someone supplied the label, "exclamation point."

Donna then shifted the focus and asked one youngster to come up and point to a word. A girl took the ruler and pointed to the capitalized, "LOOK." Donna asked how she knew that it was a word? Silently, the child pointed to the spaces on either side of the word. Donna summarized how to identify a word in print—a word is a group of letters with a space on either side. Donna asked the girl to identify the word. She had difficulty, and another child was asked to help her. This process was repeated with two more children. An important aspect of approaching written language, as noted earlier in the chapters on the development of writing, is learning how to talk about it. The idea that speech is composed of units of meaning called "words" is a very sophisticated and largely invisible structure to children until they have had many experiences with reading and writing. Shared reading is an especially good method for helping children to understand that speech written down is represented visually by words or letter sequences separated by spaces. The main strategy the children used to identify the word they pointed to was to orient themselves by going to the beginning of the sentence, repeating it from memory, and pointing to each word until they reached the one in question. The use of this strategy to identify a word reveals that the beginner has learned a great deal about directionality and the concept of words. As youngsters become increasingly familiar with particular stories, they begin to develop a sight vocabulary and can identify words out of context. This is one way that the shared-reading experience provides children with a framework for integrating their developing knowledge of story meanings and print details.

Segmenting Word Sounds

The final exercises in exploring print forms for this lesson was identifying separate word sounds. The book was still open to pages 8 and 9. Donna asked someone to find the word *came*. Once the word was identified, the youngsters were encouraged to repeat it to themselves and to name the sounds they heard. All three phonemes—the /k/, the /m/, and the long /a/—were identified. Donna turned to the next page and asked someone to find the word *tub*. After it was identified, she focused her questions related to word sounds a little differently. She asked: "What sound do you hear at the end of the word *tub*? What sound do you hear at the beginning?" The idea is to alert youngsters to the fact that in addition to visual contours, words also have a particular auditory "shape." In order to focus their attention on this aspect of oral language, children need to be able to isolate, or segment, the sounds within a word as well as to identify their locations (beginning, middle, or end) within the word.

The most important guideline to be understood from this kind of exploration of word sounds is that, unlike most other auditory exercises for beginning readers, it was done *in context*. The significance of this approach to the teaching of transcription rules cannot be overemphasized. Beginning readers are supported in their understanding of specific details about letter-sound relations when these are presented in a familiar and meaningful context. Most kindergarten programs teach the alphabet (letter names, shapes, and the sounds they represent) as a first step in teaching reading. This exercise tends to be meaningless and abstract for youngsters with little grasp of print functions, and superfluous for those with a great many experiences with books and book reading. However, both groups can benefit from opportunities to explore formal rules for converting speech to print in the context of a familiar story. The shared-reading experience provides an excellent framework for this kind of exploration.

Dramatizing the Story

At this point Donna turned to the beginning of the book and said: "If we were going to act [the story] out (much excitement and calling out of YEAAAA), if we were going to act this out, how would we know when the cow talks? (pause) which lines the cow says?" Slowly, Donna helped the children to focus on the quotation marks, which defined the lines by the different characters. Next, Donna asked: "What about the words that don't have quotation marks? Who would say that?" Having done this fairly often, most of the children responded with, "The people who are sitting down." Donna supplied the name "narrators."

organize this in small groups

The story was given two dramatic renditions. In each, different students were chosen to play the three animals and Mrs. Wishy-washy. Simple props were produced and a stage area was defined. The mud puddle was a blanket placed on one side of the group. Each of the characters was given a mask attached to a stick, which they held up to their faces. The masks were simple but descriptive: horns for the cow, a snout for the pig, and a large beak for the duck. Though there was some confusion about which parts were said by whom, the experience was exciting and satisfying for both actors and narrators.

INDEPENDENT READING:
THE LANGUAGE ARTS WORK TIME

There was much disappointment that there would not be a third dramatic rendition of the story. It was time to move into the language arts work period. In addition to the more open-ended activity time in which children explore traditional kindergarten materials (blocks, social play, art activities, and so forth), Diane organized a daily work time in which the focus was on language arts activities. A large chart was used to organize the time. The children were divided into four groups designated by color. Each group had three assigned activities, which were designated by pictures and words. On this particular day, the groups were organized as shown in Table 9.1.

As the groups settled into the work time, I followed certain youngsters and observed them move through their assigned activities. Later, I had a chance to ask Diane about tasks that were unfamiliar to me. The design and implementation of each of these independent language arts activities are described below.

Theatre.   The puppet theatre was simply a three-sided cardboard divider with a square cut out of the middle section to represent a stage. In other kindergarten classes I've observed, youngsters were often at a loss as to how to structure a puppet show. Generally, the activity degenerated into bashing hand puppets against one another in good slapstick style. In Diane's class, however, the theatre was used to enact the shared stories. Similar to the masks for *Mrs. Wishy-washy,* she had made masks or identifying cutouts for the characters from about 10 of their favorite big books. The props for each story were kept in a plastic bag stored in a box near the puppet stage. Being totally familiar with the story plot, action, and dialogue, the children were able to act out the story scripts independently. I observed one group choose a story, distribute roles, and give a performance.

Table 9.1 *Chart Organizing the Language Arts Work Time*

Group	Sequence of Activities		
RED	Theatre	Read-the-room	Writing
BLUE	Animals	Flannel Board	Big Books
GREEN	Mud Puddle	Orange Books	Read-the-room
PURPLE	Listening	Big Books	Theatre

Animals/Mud Puddle. The special activity for this work time was related to *Mrs. Wishy-washy.* Capitalizing on children's delight in images of playing in the mud, my student teacher had organized materials for two groups of children to begin creating a mural for one of the bulletin boards. One group finger painted a large sheet of paper brown (the mud puddle), while the other drew pictures of animals that would play in the mud. Going beyond the book characters, children were invited to draw and then cut out any kind of animal that appealed to them to be put in the puddle. As they finished their own activities, other children were encouraged to join this group.

Listening. A "Listening Post," as it is called in many Australian books describing read-along activities, was set up in one corner of the room. A tape recorder with five headphones allowed five youngsters to listen to a story on tape while they followed the text in a book. Multiple copies of the book come with each tape. These books are slightly smaller than normal picture books and are ideal for individual use. The taped stories were familiar to the children from the shared-reading sessions. Children could be heard repeating the story as they progressed through the tape.

Read-the-Room. The walls of Diane's classroom were filled with simple stories transferred to poster-sized paper and hung side by side so that the text was represented in proper sequence. It was clear that the children relished this particular assignment. Each of the youngsters picked up one of the yard-long pointers and began reading one wall story after another until each had read-the-room. They could be heard repeating the stories out loud. Most of these stories were either familiar chants and rhymes or stories they had read during shared-reading sessions.

Big Books. In the library corner, there was a special shelf for the big book collection. Many of these were from the collection, *The Story Box in the Classroom* (Butler, 1984). Others were teacher-made and began as read-the-room selections. Still others in this collection were large versions of class favorites from popular children's literature. The children in this group made a selection, got down on their knees on the rug with the book in front of them, and read/told the story. It was clear that big book versions of familiar stories have a certain fascination simply because of their size. The *Story Box* illustrations are especially good because of the close-up quality of the pictures.

Orange Books.   The big books also come in small, individual paperback versions whose covers are decorated at the top and bottom with a broad orange band—hence the name for this activity. Diane has multiple copies of the big book titles as well as additional stories in this size, which are stored in a rotating, spiral book-holder. The youngsters in this group picked one or two books and read in the library area alongside children who were exploring the big books.

Flannel Board.   In addition to the flannel board, there are several small bags of flannel props and characters for storytelling. Again, modeling themselves on the stories that Diane has told them, each child in this group chose a particular bag and retold his or her version of the story to the others in the group.

Writing.   Youngsters assigned to the writing area went to get their individual writing folders and brought them to the writing table. These folders were for storing their work-in-progress. The children's work reflected the range of writing behaviors described earlier. I watched as Diane worked with this group of children. In addition to oral discussions of children's pictures and story ideas, Diane focused on helping youngsters move toward early phonemic and/or letter-name spelling. When asked how to write a word, Diane would repeat it slowly and direct the child to listen for beginning, middle, and end sounds. Some youngsters no longer needed Diane to model this process for them. They could be heard repeating to themselves the words they wanted to spell. Over the course of the year, most of the youngsters in Diane's group extended their writing repertoire to include the use of the alphabetic principle and to produce invented spellings for key words in their stories.

The variety of activities and the interest and focus of the children as they moved through their assigned tasks were wonderful to observe. Since my visit took place in the spring of the year, the children had become remarkably independent in their ability to guide themselves through their activities, and only occasional reminders were needed to refocus a stray youngster. The entire period lasted about 30 to 40 minutes. As the children finished their assigned tasks (using approximately half of the period), they moved on to things of their choice. They could return to a previous activity or try something that had not been assigned to their group.

The value of this kind of activity period in relation to early literacy learning needs to be underscored. The emphasis was on providing time for youngsters to function as independent storytellers, readers, and writers. The method, derived, as noted, from the handover principle, emphasized youngsters being active producers and translators of texts. As the repertoire of books and texts explored during the guided-reading sessions expanded, the children's repertoire of independent reading choices increased. What was very visible, when observing this work time, was that every child thought of himself or herself as a reader and could handle a variety of text materials independently. Approaching books, as these youngsters understood it, was not confined to providing an exact rendition (a voice-print match) of a text. Rather, it was retelling a story in one's own words, reading story illustrations, exploring narratives in dramatic form, and creating one's own renditions and extensions of story ideas in pictures and words. What was most impressive, then, was the sense of "I can do" in relation to books and stories, and the feeling everyone communicated that reading was one of the most delightful activities in the world.

CHILDREN'S READING REPERTOIRE

Children's reading development can be described as evolving in three general stages (Cochrane, Cochrane, Scalena, & Buchanan, 1984; Reading in Junior Classes, 1985):

1. Emergent reader
   - Interested in handling books
   - Notices environmental print
   - Names pictures in books
   - Reconstructs own versions of stories in familiar books
   - Can pick out own name
   - Can identify certain words or letters
   - Enjoys repeating chants and rhymes

2. Early reader
   - Understands print is the base for deriving meaning
   - Relies heavily on author's print when reconstructing story
   - Wants to read to people
   - Can identify familiar words in a variety of contexts

- Has command of key elements of story structures (for example, repetition form, fairy tales, problem stories)

3. Fluent reader
   - Builds on previous stages
   - Can process print details automatically
   - Can handle a variety of print forms independently (prose, poetry, TV listings, menus, and so forth)
   - Can read at a rate appropriate to the print form

This sequence describes the vertical growth of reading abilities. Developing readers slowly expand their abilities to handle greater quantities and varieties of print materials and to process transcription details with ever-increasing accuracy and speed.

Reading development, however, also moves along a horizontal continuum, a movement that provides an index of an individual's reading behaviors at one point in time. For example, though I am considered a fluent reader and am able to handle many print forms with ease, my ability to handle legal texts, as noted, is limited at best. I would probably be considered an emergent, or at most an early, reader in this area. With more experience and with help from people who are fluent with this category of knowledge, I could become fluent in my ability to process legal texts. Emergent or early reading, then, when applied to my situation, defines the approach I would bring to unfamiliar text types.

By the same token, youngsters whose reading behaviors are described largely as emergent can exhibit fluency with certain materials. For example, at two, Giti exhibited a fluency in identifying McDonald's logos, as well as her name and the names of her family (Baghban, 1984). In her case, fluency described the fact that she was practicing and mastering the rapid discrimination of a limited group of print samples. This kind of practice is important to support Giti's confidence as a reader and to confirm to her that this approach to print is an important part of what it takes to grow as a reader.

In addition to describing the move from less mature to more mature reading behavior, the terms *emergent, early,* and *fluent* describe approaches to written material that are exercised by both immature and mature readers. To recognize that literacy learning can be described by growth in both vertical and horizontal directions underscores the importance of designing reading programs that support an individual youngster's range of reading behaviors. The three-pronged approach outlined at the beginning of this chapter is an example of a program that builds on the youngster's developing abilities.

Most school districts in our country have instituted all-day kindergarten programs. Preschool classes for four-year-olds are being phased in in New

York City. In the coming decade, the rest of the nation is likely to follow this trend. That these programs can be highly beneficial to N–K youngsters, especially in the area of language learning, is incontestable. We need to achieve consistency between how young children learn and how we teach. Formal teaching methods and materials are inappropriate in classrooms for these ages. Children are writing and reading at four and five, and many of them, having been at it for sometime, are well on their way to mastering certain forms of written language. Almost without exception, formal programs ignore these developments. It is up to teachers and administrators to look at what children already know and to build programs that extend their knowledge rather than undermine it. This perspective of literacy programs for young children is the focus of the last part of this book, in which problems with the formal approach to teaching reading and writing in the primary grades are described.

Part IV

THE PRIMARY YEARS

10

Reading and Writing in the Early Grades

Historical Perspectives

I canvass my graduate students at the beginning of the semester about their beliefs regarding teaching and learning in the elementary years. Almost without exception, adults agree that beginning with the first grade, children need to "get down to work." While an emphasis on developing social skills and on more creative and open-ended activities may be appropriate prior to these years, the elementary years are a time for mastering basic skills in reading, writing, and math. My students' attitudes, of course, mirror exactly what most of the rest of our society, including both parents and teachers, tend to believe about how to educate the elementary ages.

Moreover, students express the view that the methods for teaching the "getting down to work" program should be a no-nonsense approach. The teacher-directed, formal educational model is recognizable by anyone who has spent the first through sixth grades in almost any of our public or private elementary institutions. Teachers do the telling and are mainly concerned with covering the syllabus by predetermined dates. Children learn, in this view, not by reasoning from experience, but rather by imitating what is told to them.

The fact that this attitude is so pervasive is not surprising when we look at elementary schooling in a historical context. This perspective of teaching/learning processes has its roots in the nineteenth century when the elementary school system began in this country. Historically, this was a time of tremendous expansion to the west, with the result that families and friends were separated by large distances. Keeping in touch was done not by telephone, but by writing letters. Reading newspapers was essential to keep informed about significant events in a large country, and the need to be informed was underscored by the increasing size of the voting population. Though women's suffrage did not become law until 1920, the numbers of men who were voters expanded significantly during the nineteenth century. The democratic political process, with its emphasis on individual decision making, requires that its voters be informed about issues and candidates for office. Until the advent of mass media, the primary sources of information were newspapers and journals. In a broad sense, then, our geography and our political system figured importantly in shaping the country's eventual goal of developing 100 percent literacy in the population.

THE ROOTS OF THE ELEMENTARY SCHOOL SYSTEM

More specifically, though, it was the expansion of the economic system that initiated the relatively swift growth of our public school system. The Industrial Revolution and the gradual shift from an agrarian to a largely manufacturing economy brought a need for workers who could read and write. Clerks were needed to take care of the paper work surrounding the buying, selling, and transporting of large quantities of products over long distances. Processing of orders as well as keeping the accounts required a minimum competence in the three R's. Parents recognized that to be economically competitive, young people entering the work force must be capable of handling written symbols, both words and numbers.

The most economical way to achieve literacy on a broad scale was to create schools in which the three R's were the central focus. Tutoring, a traditional method for educating young children, was available only to the well-to-do. In Europe, when youngsters were educated in groups, it was generally done at boarding schools. The expense of boarding schools, and the need for farm families to have their youngsters at home to help with the daily chores, precluded the development of this kind of institution in America on anything but a very limited scale.

The people, mostly women, who became teachers tended to be a sturdy group. In the beginning, they were hired and paid by the parents of a school community, and they lived with the families of their students on a rotating basis. "Schoolmarms," as they came to be called, were given a job definition that included rules of behavior outside as well as inside the school. In their private lives, they were to represent models of socially correct behavior.

Parents tended to feel that those teachers who inspired fear in their students were most successful. Corporal punishment was viewed as a useful way to motivate students, either socially or academically, and its use was encouraged. The prevalent view that such practices in working with young students have become outmoded is far from the truth. According to an article on the front page of the *New York Times* (Schmidt, 1987), 41 states still had laws at that time that permitted school administrators to use corporal punishment in dealing with students.

In 1892, Joseph Rice, a pediatrician who made a study of elementary schools, traveled to 36 cities and observed 1200 teachers in a period of 6 months. Not only did he examine teaching methods, finding them almost uniformly mechanical and utterly dominated by boring and/or difficult texts, but he also investigated the views of teachers and administrators regarding the governing of children's social behavior (Rice, 1892/1969). In the latter area, Rice reported that a principal, when asked whether children in a particular classroom were allowed to turn their heads, answered: "Why should they look behind them when the teacher is in front of them" (p. 32).

Throughout the nineteenth century, then, classroom social structure tended to be restrictive and forbidding. Work was to be done while sitting quietly. Social interactions with peers were rarely permitted. Talking was allowed only when solicited by the teacher and then only to provide monosyllabic answers or memorized recitations of assigned material (Cuban, 1984). Quite apart from the need for safety and efficiency in organizing the actions of so many in a limited space, the main motivation for constructing this kind of class community was to restrict normal social interactions as much as possible. The assumption was that learning, or intellectual development, could proceed most effectively when the social context of the educational experience was either eliminated or kept to a minimum. Further, if it did intrude, that is, if students were in any way uncooperative, such behavior was to be dealt with swiftly and severely. This attitude resulted in the shaping of an institution in which social relations and teaching methods bore more similarities to a military model of living and learning than to a community in which knowledge about printed symbols was the central focus.

Teaching methods were similarly unresponsive to young students' patterns of learning. On the front page of the July 12, 1826 issue of the *Hampshire Gazette,* published in Northampton, Massachusetts, there was an editorial critical of then popular methods of teaching reading (Popular education, 1826). The writer began with an attack on the uselessness of teaching grammar to children. Since it is a highly abstract perspective of language, the author noted, it can be appreciated only by scholars. The child who learns "new names" for words such as verbs and nouns and "a parade of definitions" thinks he is acquiring great knowledge ". . . while in fact he is learning nothing."

The next items to come under attack were the materials used to teach reading, which, according to the author, were highly inappropriate because they were incomprehensible to young people. In those days, a published reader was made up of excerpts of classic examples of adult literature. The method then (as now) was to read round robin style, with each student reading a few sentences. The author recalled with humor how students would read this material, making "ridiculous blunders," and resorting to a sing-song, monotonous delivery. Like the teaching of grammar, the teaching of reading, the writer reported, was largely a matter of exposing students to subjects and ideas that were not appropriate to their age and understanding.

Finally, the writer pleaded for the methods and materials for teaching reading to be made, above all, intelligible to young people:

> Much of the ignorance of the community is to be traced to this kind of learning. . . . The abused mind still gives this testimony to its intrinsic dignity, that it cannot be interested in what it does not understand. Words, that neither teach nor signify anything to it, must be dull; they ought to be dull. . . . There cannot be a worse habit for the mind, if not the heart, than to be content with an equivocal, half way knowledge of what is studied, or read, or heard.

According to this editorial writer, then, the typical elementary school program was not designed with young learners in mind. To expose youngsters to material that was beyond their experience and understanding was to ensure a lack of interest in schoolwork and, as the author put it, to create a negative attitude toward learning in general. The writer proposed that educators change this "evil" and design materials suited to the interests and experiences of young students. Such views were innovative at the time, but ultimately they became the standard by which reading material was chosen for beginners.

Such changes pointed in a pedagogically sound direction. The published materials that grew out of these perspectives of learning to read began to infiltrate elementary classrooms at the beginning of this century. In the past 50 years, moreover, published reading programs, designed in content and style with the child in mind, have proliferated dramatically. Their growth, however, has not transformed our elementary classrooms, as the *Hampshire Gazette* editorialist hoped they would, into places where reading and learning to read are interesting, much less riveting, events. Indeed, if the design of primers of past times erred on the side of complexity, the design of early readers that have come into widespread use in this century err on the side of oversimplification. Add to this the lingering of the teaching-as-telling methods as well as a socially restrictive classroom community, and we have an elementary education system that is more similar to, than different from, the nineteenth-century version.

DICK AND JANE AND SPOT AND PUFF

I began first grade in 1944 in a small suburban school in Pennsylvania. I was eager to begin reading, and I was thrilled with my first primer, which had pictures of children about my age, their parents, and their pets. In this school the first and second grades were in one room, a total of 25 students, nearly evenly divided between the two grades. The first grade reading lesson was conducted with all of us moving from our desks to the two rows of chairs that faced the blackboard. Our teacher would put new words on the board, point to them, say them, and instruct us to repeat them after her. I could hardly believe the process was so simple. I looked; I said; I remembered. In no time at all, I could open my book and read any page. Such independence, however, was discouraged. We were instructed to read this material at reading time, each of us reading a sentence. We reread the same material a couple of times until everyone had at least one turn at reading aloud. The stories were about the now famous, or infamous, Dick and Jane and their pets, Spot the dog and Puff the cat.

At that point in time, this teaching system represented an innovative approach—the look-say method—for identifying words. The procedure for beginner readers was for the teacher to write the words on the board, to repeat them slowly, and to have students repeat them. The strategy was to develop a sight vocabulary by having students memorize word configurations. The other popular, and more traditional, approach for instructing beginners was the use of phonics, with its emphasis on teaching children to identify words by sound-to-letter relationships. In both approaches, the process of teaching beginner readers was understood as simply a task of helping them to identify words. Regardless of the method for teaching word identification, the reading materials used with each system were carefully edited to conform to the repertoire of words that students had been prepared to read. Hence the evolution of the very truncated "Dick and Jane" type stories in which the characters did little more than "run" and "play."

Far from improving the teaching of reading, these kinds of texts have tended to contribute to the difficulties experienced by both mainstream and nonmainstream youngsters in school reading programs. Looking back at my first grade classmates, it is easy to understand what separated those who could handle the material from those who couldn't. In this small, relatively homogeneous community, the majority of students came from middle-class homes in which family storytimes were a regular activity. I visited the homes of most of my classmates, and their array of books and toys was similar to mine. Story reading was a part of our daily routines. Moreover, our parents read for pleasure and to "get things done." The "Dick and Jane" stories were simple for us, but we found them unappealing. The texts added very little to our developing knowledge of books and stories, except the fact that some types could be excruciatingly dull.

The students who couldn't handle the program were the farm children whose parents were illiterate. These classmates appeared to be confused by the look-say lessons, and they stumbled through the round robin reading sessions. Undoubtedly, their understanding of story form suffered from a lack of exposure to books and story reading. The Dick and Jane primers tended to make little contribution to these youngsters' understanding of storybooks because they did not use phrasing, vocabulary, or narrative forms typical of storytelling/writing. If these are the first and only stories to which nonmainstream students are exposed on a steady basis, then they have limited opportunities to come to grips with book language and story structure.

As we progressed through the grades, the approach to teaching reading remained pretty much the same. The readers included increasingly complex material, which most of us could read with ease and fluency. For those who had difficulty in the first grade, things got worse as time went on. The system of two grades per classroom continued through the fifth and sixth grades. At this point, it was necessary to read not only the reader, but the history book as well as the geography and science texts. While the teacher worked with the other grade, we were given reading assignments from these books and required to answer the questions at the end of the chapters. After the assigned work had been completed, we were allowed to go to the class library and take a book to read. The biographies about famous people in American history intrigued many of us. The narratives were vivid and rich in human detail, the way good historical fiction should be. I remember sharing what I had read (outside of school) with my girl friends. We gave each other recommendations about what to read and compared the thoughts and feelings that the lives of these people evoked in us. Often, we were inspired and dreamed of becoming a nurse, like Clara Barton, or organizing a home for the needy (especially children), like Jane Addams. The less able readers rarely had time to explore the class library, since they hardly ever finished their assigned work. It is doubtful, though, that they would have been able to read such materials independently.

In classrooms today, the reading lesson, now preceded and extended by numerous drill sheets, continues to lack challenge for the able students and to baffle youngsters who are at risk academically. The problems with current teaching methods are identified in the following analysis of current lessons as they are presented in nearly all basal reading programs.

THE GUIDED–READING LESSON

A typical guided-reading lesson in a basal text for the primary grade covers both comprehension and word analysis skills. The session begins with the teacher asking predictive- and speculative-type questions about the text.

Usual questions are: "What do you think this story might be about? From the title? From the pictures?" This discussion is followed by students reading one page at a time, aloud in the first grade and silently after that. The teacher continues to ask questions before and after the reading of each page. These questions are designed to check youngsters' comprehension of story facts, as well as to solicit their personal observations and hypotheses about what will happen next. In addition, attention is given to word structures: examples of particular vowel sounds, prefixes, suffixes, or whatever happens to be the special skills focus of that day or week. The exploration of print rules and patterns does not, of course, have to do with the unfolding of the narrative. Further, these regular interruptions intrude upon the pleasure in reading and the understanding of the story.

With some variation in types of questions and their quantity and timing, this is the approach used for exploring stories in the basal readers for the early grades. As a way of evaluating these methods, let's compare them with the design for teaching reading outlined in Chapter 9. Every program, it was stated, should include three parts: (1) conceptual preparation through reading aloud by the teacher, (2) guided-reading sessions, and (3) independent reading time. When measured against these criteria, the basal programs fail not so much because of what they cover, but because of what they don't include in their teaching design. The fact that steps (1) and (3) have been almost entirely eliminated from current basal reading programs is more than unfortunate; it is tragic. Listening to the teacher read aloud is the process by which beginners, especially those who do not come from mainstream families, are introduced to book language and story structures. Further, it places the emphasis in the teaching/learning of reading where it belongs—on the pleasure and the joy of exploring literature and other written material.

The fact that beginner reading material in basal texts is not used for reading aloud by the teacher or for shared-book experiences is not surprising when we consider the nature of these stories. Because of the controlled vocabularies on which these narratives are built, the characters, like Dick and Jane of past decades, do little more than run and play, or walk and talk. Constructed for the purpose of practicing words, primer stories are not written to be read for the literary value of the narrative.

Overlooking the shared-book experience, moreover, presents other problems for beginners. Stories are presented as puzzles that youngsters must piece together for themselves without the benefit of shared-reading experiences. The teaching method is to require that children produce an exact voice-print match (to read the text exactly as it is written) on their first try. In this approach, then, beginners are asked to approach an unfamiliar story and to read it for the first time for meaning and accuracy. The procedure is identical to asking youngsters to produce standard spelling and punctuation in their first efforts at writing. In effect, the basal programs have totally over-looked the emergent literacy phase of development. The design of programs for the beginner continues to be governed by the erroneous assumption that learning to read is simply a matter of decoding words.

If the guided-reading lesson is too abstract and demanding for beginners with little book/story experience, it is too confining for those who are able to meet the expectations to decode/encode primer stories on the first try. These students suffer from the lack of challenge in these programs, which are based on devoting an entire reading time to the guided-reading experience. Not only are these youngsters capable of reading more challenging material, but they are also capable of reading independently, an experience that is not regularly scheduled in the reading periods. As described in Chapter 9, all youngsters benefit from having time to independently explore familiar texts, whether by reading, re-telling, dramatizing, or using read-along materials.

The basal materials adapt easily to the grouping methods that, even when I was in the early grades, were associated with teaching reading. Every class still has at least two, or sometimes three or four, reading groups determined by ability. The reading materials are sequenced, not by grade, but by reading level (determined by the complexity of the material). What this means is that, in any single classroom, the faster group or groups are further ahead in the text than their slower peers. Typical of this kind of organization is the names that teachers use to distinguish one group from another. The tigers and the lions, the daisies and the roses, or, in our current era, names of favorite TV characters may be used. As most of us remember, these names did nothing to camouflage the fact that one group consisted of better readers than did another.

The rationale for this procedure is the same today as it was when I was in elementary school. Grouping for reading instruction is meant to meet the individual needs of students. Those who can move ahead with ease should be able to read further ahead in the book than their less able peers who will cover the same material at a later date. Pace, then, is the major criterion upon which group divisions are made. Such an approach, though, in no way meets the needs of youngsters with less book experience, who require shared-book sessions and predictable materials to help them to approach new texts. Also, as noted, this approach eliminates true challenges for the more able readers by not providing a variety of text materials or time for independent reading.

The basal materials are built upon a limited understanding of learning processes. Each reading selection is viewed as a one-shot experience. Stories are consumed rather than savored. In this approach, learning to read is per-ceived as a linear process. Each story represents a building block. As one block gets piled on top of another, the learner presumably moves closer to a certain level of reading competence. To return to a story already read represents a step backward in this process. To linger over a story that is especially appropriate or appealing to a particular class group is seen as a waste of time and as interfering with progress toward a predetermined goal. This attitude undermines the fact that reading is pleasurable and functional. We read stories for the joy of immersing ourselves in a fictional world. The fact that basal materials consistently overlook or give second priority to this basic reason for reading, and therefore for learning to read, not only weakens their impact but also produces a negative attitude toward the entire school reading experience.

Ironically, the creators of basal programs often say that this is not what is intended. They protest that the teaching guides always suggest some fun follow-ups to the guided-reading lesson, in which students are to be encouraged to reread a selection, to respond through drawings, and so forth. What is misunderstood, however, is the stultifying effect that the nearly monolithic use of the guided-reading approach has on students' responses to school reading lessons. The guided lesson, by definition, is teacher directed. It begins and ends with teachers outlining and defining each step. To suggest, at certain points, that students show more creativity and initiative in their responses to reading material, poses an expectation for which they have no preparation. Ways and means for relating to literature through independent reading, acting out stories, and composing one's own stories, to cite a few examples, must be regularly modeled and encouraged if they are to become a regular part of students' repertoire of responses to reading material.

The basal programs have tended to strengthen the hold that the formal, nineteenth-century teaching model has on the elementary classroom. The teacher guides provide very detailed descriptions of how each moment of each reading lesson should be conducted. They tend to be written in the kind of prescriptive language of how-to manuals. The teacher is rarely asked to invent or to elaborate. In some programs, the manuals provide the script that the teacher and pupils are to repeat without variation. In the profession, such programs have come to be known as "teacher-proof." The idea is that it doesn't matter who the teacher is because the programs can be relied upon to do the teaching. They represent the ultimate in the imitation theory of learning. Teachers and students simply repeat the script that has been set out for them, and they do it again and again until the performance is perfect. To a greater or lesser extent, then, basal programs tend to rob teachers of their initiative and to undermine their professional stature as designers of programs for their students, the job that they have been trained to do. Not surprisingly, when these materials are implemented as the exclusive program, youngsters are similarly sapped of their initiative and independence in their responses to reading activities.

A COLLABORATIVE APPROACH
TO LITERACY TEACHING

The nearly exclusive use of formal teaching methods in elementary reading programs is not surprising when we consider that it is an extension of the educational tradition that has shaped our elementary classrooms. What we are confronting is not just decades of the use of basal programs; rather, it is an educational legacy built upon social and academic systems inherited from another era. The legacy continues to shape our views and to result in the production of ineffective literacy programs. Teaching by drilling learners on bits and pieces of written language rules and skills, in a classroom in which social interaction is confined to students answering adults' questions, is the way it has been done for nearly two centuries.

In the past 10 to 15 years, researchers have gone into the homes and schools and gathered data regarding teaching/learning situations using ethnographic research perspectives. The special focus of this kind of research is the examination and documentation of all of the influences that are a part of any educational experience. As discussed, literary learning in the home is intimately connected to the social situations in which infants and toddlers are engaged daily and that highlight functions of oral and written language. This same perspective has been brought to classrooms, where the effort has been to describe the social and academic contexts that surround teaching and learning in elementary programs.

Similar to discoveries of the significance of family social context in the preschool child's language development, researchers have documented interrelations among social and academic programs in the classroom. As the data accumulate, guidelines for educators of children in the early grades emerge with greater and greater clarity. Of these, the most important are those already described as central to collaborative approach to teaching: taking the child's perspective, assuming that children come to school with literacy knowledge, assessing what children do know, and building programs from there.

The most concentrated and, to date, best documented descriptions of what it means to teach collaboratively in elementary school settings comes from the research on writing process programs. Donald Graves and Lucy Calkins, to name the two most influential researchers in this field, have provided teachers with unique and extremely useful studies of writing programs from kindergarten through the grades (Calkins, 1983, 1986; Graves, 1983). Additionally, other researchers and writers have provided descriptions of whole language programs in which the process approach is applied to teaching reading as well as writing (Goodman, 1986; Holdaway, 1984; Hornsby & Sukarna, with Parry, 1986; Newman, 1985; Schwartz, 1988).

The commendable and largely successful effort of reading and writing process research has been to offer a model of school literacy programs in which language learning is given a social context: The adult/student relationship is redefined as a collaboration, and student-to-student exchanges are regarded as important to classroom life and learning experiences. Additionally, literacy learning is described as a developmental process. In this view, the behaviors of the beginner, though they differ significantly from the actions of the mature reader and writer, are recognized as crucial to the learning process. These social and intellectual perspectives of literacy learning have already made a significant contribution to revising literacy teaching. They represent precisely the kind of guide needed for transforming the traditional, formal approach to elementary education to a collaborative social and intellectual experience. The most influential teaching/learning moments, as we are coming to understand them, are those in which both teachers and students raise questions, share views, and search for solutions. The greatest challenge to educators responsible for the early grades is to erode the continued influence of the formal educational model and to achieve consistency between how teachers teach and how children learn. Descriptions of some of these possibilities for the early grades are the focus of the next two chapters.

11

Encouraging Young Writers

Creative writing is the label used to describe traditional writing programs in the elementary years. Sessions begin with the teacher choosing the topic, which is often an uncreative standby such as "What I Did on My Summer Vacation" or "My First Day of School." Other typical choices are designed to stretch students' imaginations by suggesting an unusual angle for thinking about something. Titles such as "How It Feels to Be a Stapler" or "My Life as a Fish" would fit into this group. In recent years, cards with pictures designed to stimulate writing have been published as "story starters." Sometimes these cards have an unfinished sentence printed alongside the picture so that the first words amount to a fill-in-the-blank type exercise. One of the misguided assumptions underlying the adult choice of topic is that many children don't have anything to write about. Another perception about writing that underlies this practice is that creativity is generated by imposing topics on students. The evidence most teachers cite to support their actions is that the invitation to "write about anything you want to" brings louder groans and less productivity than the assignment of a topic.

In the traditional program, the most predictable aspect of prewriting discussions tends to focus on how long the finished product has to be. Anticipating that many students will produce a few sentences and claim they have exhausted their interest in or experience with the topic, teachers often succumb to this mechanization of the writing task and specify the number of sentences, paragraphs, or space-on-the-page as a minimum length. They know they can count on just that amount of print from the less interested members of the class. Though we wouldn't consider asking youngsters to sit down and read a book without a great deal of support, we regularly ask youngsters to produce compositions with little guidance or encouragement.

Writing time takes place in an absolutely silent room, an atmosphere, it is believed, that is needed for concentration. The teacher generally sits at the desk and often welcomes the chance to take care of some paper work. At the end of the period, student productions are collected for the teacher to read at a later time. Writing periods are scheduled on an average of once every other week or, when there are other more important activities, once a month (or less). It is assumed that learning to write, unlike learning to read, requires very little actual practice.

The real agony begins when the papers are returned. Ask college students what they remember about their earliest writing efforts, and they will tell you that it was the red marks that appeared all over their papers. What is most tragic in this writing program is that the focus on form, or transcription, tends to obscure entirely an appreciation of content. College students report that never, or only rarely, did their elementary teachers comment on what they wrote. It becomes apparent in listening to these young adults recount their early writing experiences that what they wrote was important to them. Most can recall specific ideas or experiences they were attempting to describe in one of their first compositions that was returned with marks correcting punctuation and spelling. The message, which students learn very quickly, is that form is important and content is negligible. As a result, they begin to use safe sentences, comprising words they are confident they can spell: "I like school." "I like to play." The shock comes when students get to high school and college and find that a mechanical response to writing assignments is considered inadequate. Now they are expected to think, to imagine, and to possess a certain competence in fulfilling writing assignments, a form of communication they have had limited opportunities to practice and few occasions to discuss or share with anyone except an unresponsive teacher.

Given these circumstances, it is not surprising that we continue to encounter many undergraduate and graduate students whose writing skills are limited and who readily admit that they feel totally inadequate in this area of language learning. What is surprising is that we have tended not to connect adult attitudes and children's early classroom experiences as being largely responsible for later difficulties.

THE WRITING WORKSHOP

As noted in the previous chapter, Donald Graves (1983), along with colleagues at the University of New Hampshire (Hansen, 1987; Newkirk & Atwell, 1982), has researched, documented, and written about a process approach to teaching writing. Lucy Calkins (1983, 1986), originally a member of the New Hampshire research team, has continued her research in New York City, where she has developed the "Teachers College Writing Project," which educates teachers and administrators throughout the city and, in the summers, from all over the world.

With the leadership of these researchers, a quiet but very exciting reformation of literacy programs has been taking place in schools all over the country. The following paragraphs summarize significant contributions this research has made to our understanding of how children learn to write and how teachers can contribute to the process.

Components of the Writing Process

Topic Choice.   In contrast to the traditional program, a hallmark of the process approach to writing is that students choose the topics they write about. This prewriting task can be approached in many ways. Many teachers lead group brainstorming sessions in which students enumerate possible topics. Individuals can record those topics that suggest a story that they would like to explore in writing. The can keep this list in their writing folder and add to it as possibilities suggest themselves. The writing program begins, then, by putting the responsibility for topic choice squarely in the hands of the writer. The teacher's role, especially for youngsters who are having difficulty, is to help students think about their experiences with life and literature as sources of inspiration.

Drafting.   As noted, the most counterproductive aspect of traditional writing programs is the almost exclusive focus on form. Drafting is based on the concept that a single piece of writing evolves over time rather than springing fully formed from the first attempt. This is as true for experienced as for inexperienced writers. What is mysterious is why this process, which is usually introduced to high school or college students, has not been considered an important step for beginners. If one were to choose the single most significant contribution of writing process to the transformation of teaching, it would probably be the recognition that children's writings must evolve and that first drafts must be responded to differently than final versions.

Revising.   Further, revising or rewriting is not always a part of every effort to commit thoughts to paper. The ephemeral quality of children's productions must be respected. Enthusiasms shift and change over the course of a week, even a day, and what seemed riveting one moment may not be so the next. Not everything is meant to be treated with equal depth and seriousness. Indeed, part of the process of choice of topic continues to be played out in the drafting and revising processes as youngsters explore an interest by expanding its possibilities on paper. As often as not, they tend to discover that what seemed like a good idea at one point is not something they wish to pursue. When revision does become a part of the process, it too needs to be presented in stages. Beginners revise by simply adding on to a story, while more experienced writers can be encouraged to expand descriptions, change sections around, and/or rewrite certain parts with an eye to improving their writing techniques (Calkins, 1986; Graves, 1983).

Conferencing.   Rivaling the importance of drafting to revolutionizing writing programs is the emphasis placed on the social context in which writing takes place. No longer considered a solo flight from title to ending, the evolution of a piece of writing takes place within a network of encouragement and feedback from adults and peers. The writing time is designed as a workshop precisely because the intent is for pieces of writing to be shared with others as they evolve, not just when they are completed. The teacher leads the way by circulating during the writing time and conferencing with youngsters. Initially, the teacher needs to listen, "really listen," as Calkins (1986) puts it, to what the youngster is eager to share. Listening is followed by the teacher's posing questions and comments that adopt the child's perspective of the work. And just as adults are the mediators between children and the construction of story meanings at the read-aloud session, so they are mediators between children and their writing creations. Conferencing between students can also provide the same kind of help and encouragement.

Sharing.   Similar to conferencing is the sharing session at the end of a writing period. After writing for 30 to 40 minutes, the group gathers, and one or two youngsters read their work-in-progress or a finished product. Classmates respond to the writer and the writing: "I didn't understand the part about. . . ." "Why did you make the dragon green?" "I went on a camping trip, too, but we didn't see any raccoons." Because similar perspectives of life and stories tend to be shared by students of the same age, classmates provide one of the best sources of feedback. Of deeper significance, however, is the fact of sharing itself. In the traditional program, only the teacher reads student compositions. This procedure is inconsistent with the fact that real writing serves particular functions and purposes. Learning to write has as much to do with understanding who you are writing for as what you want to say. Young children need to have the invisible process of reader/listener reaction made visible for them; they need to hear what their friends think about what they have written. In short, just as young children learn conversation conventions by getting feedback from their partners, so young writers can learn what their writing means to others when they share what they have written.

Editing.   Editing is appropriate only for youngsters who have already had much experience drafting and only for those pieces that the writer chooses to bring to this level. The two areas that generally need the most attention are punctuation and spelling. Punctuation is very much integrated with composing. The only transcription clues the reader has about how to read strings of words are the capital letters, commas, periods, question marks, exclamation points, and so forth used to divide the text into meaningful sections. Reading writing aloud is the best method for determining where to include these marks, and student reading of drafts out loud represents a central focus of conferences and sharing sessions.

Youngsters in the early grades tend to be letter-name or transitional spellers (discussed below). In such writing, identifying the word is rarely a problem because these versions are very close to standard forms. One way to have students take an active role in editing their spelling is to ask them to circle those words they think may be incorrect. Generally youngsters' visual memory for words that they use in their writing has developed to a point where they can recognize that certain words are spelled incorrectly even though they can't produce the standard version. However, this awareness generally indicates that they are ready to take the final steps in mastering conventional spelling for these words. The important thing to remember is that a concern for spelling must not intrude upon the flow of writing. As a result, learning to spell as a specific focus needs to be scheduled separately from writing workshops.

Organization of the Classroom

As is true of all class activities, careful and consistent management procedures are necessary to guide class groups through the writing workshop. The idea is to organize rules and expectations for moving and talking in a way that helps youngsters to become increasingly independent in shaping their writing time. Writing folders for storing work-in-progress need to be available for each student. Writing materials such as paper, pencils and pens, staplers, Scotch tape, and other implements need to be kept in clearly marked containers and made readily available during writing times. Because children naturally talk about what they are doing as they write, a steady hum is usually heard during the workshop time. Youngsters move about the room to share with each other and to get needed materials related to writing.

Students who are disruptive and unable to handle the independence usually have had little contact with reading and writing on a steady basis outside of school, or are afraid to risk putting things on paper because they "don't know how to spell," the skill that in many children's minds is synonymous with writing. Students in the former category often need to talk, to become more immersed in literature, and/or to draw before they begin writing. For some students, this could take nearly a year. Youngsters in the latter category need regular reassurance that what they write and not how they write is the central focus of the writing workshop.

Finally, writing periods must be scheduled on a regular basis, preferably daily. Though most primary programs assign a large block of time to the reading program, writing is generally squeezed in at irregular intervals. At the very least, common sense tells us that if it requires regular practice to become a fluent reader, it doesn't require anything less to become a fluent writer.

Teachers as Writers

One of the reasons many of us have had such difficulty in responding to children's composing is that we were ill at ease with our own writing abilities. Writing process teachers report, on the other hand, that their understanding of children's work evolves as a direct outcome of their personal efforts to develop as writers. Such testimony must be taken very seriously. Until we have raised an entire generation of youngsters on writing process and these students are ready to move into the ranks of teachers, we must provide our preservice and practicing teachers with opportunities to become active and comfortable communicators through writing.

TRANSITIONAL SPELLING

The ability to transcribe thoughts and ideas into written form begins to be an automatic response during the middle and later elementary years. Spelling, along with punctuation, and sentence and paragraph formation begin to take their places as written language frames and, given adequate reading and writing process programs, become a part of the students' writing repertoire.

As noted in Chapter 8, most youngsters in the early grades are transitional spellers. The transitional phase reflects the fact that students are becoming readers and are exposed to print on a daily basis. This exposure reveals that alphabetic strategies are not the only rules that govern word spellings. A good example of transitional spelling is the first draft of a Halloween composition by seven-year-old Eric:

> I was led into a darck cave. Before I new it a Big baer Jumpt at me. and then a nother baer jumpt at me. Then a was trapped. Where could I go?

Eric's command of conventional features of print is extensive. Sentence/phrase divisions are clear; capitals begin four of the five sentences and are used in the second sentence to lend drama, apparently, to the action described ("a Big baer Jumpt"). Word boundaries are understood except for the separation of *a* and *nother*—an understandable division given the common use of *a* as an article. Further, Eric reveals that he uses several strategies to help him spell words whose orthographic features he has not yet mastered.

> *darck/dark:* overgeneralizing a common spelling feature; *ck* often represents the /k/ sound after a vowel (pick, duck, tack, rock).

new/knew: confusion of homophones (words identical in sound); other typical examples are too/to/two, hear/here, and so on.

baer/bear: all the letters are represented but they are in the wrong order. (Note the *ae* and *ea* can both represent the long /a/ sound.)

jumpt/jumped: use of letter-name strategy; in this case the *ed* is pronounced /t/. (Note, however, that *trapped,* pronounced *trapt,* is spelled correctly, suggesting that Eric is aware of the *ed* marker for past tense but his implementation of this rule has not yet become automatic. Such slips are typical occurrences in both children's and adults' writing drafts.)

In contrast to the more limited strategies of letter-name spellers (see Chapter 8), Eric has added some important principles to his spelling repertoire. Especially helpful is the fact that he has begun to discriminate certain letter groups and sequences as typical of English spelling, although they are not based on sound-symbol relations. Such an expansion suggests that Eric's understanding of English orthography has become more sophisticated. It also suggests that he would benefit from exploring games in which players manipulate letters to form words (scrambled words, word strings, crossword puzzles, Scrabble, to name a few). As Hodges (1981) points out:

> Spelling "consciousness," a sensitivity to the appearance of written words, does not occur automatically. Like other aspects of spelling ability, this skill . . . develops over time, [and] games and activities that focus the child's attention on the spellings of words in print contribute to its development. (p. 21)

There are literally dozens of games in which children must manipulate letter sequences as they search for combinations and permutations of letter groups that form new words. Many, in fact, are described in Hodges' useful booklet, *Learning to Spell* (1981).

Another example of transitional spelling is from eight-year-old Shannon who lives in Chicago and who enclosed her story of a pirate adventure in a letter to her aunt, a teacher in New York City (see Figure 11.1). In the letter that accompanied the story, she described her pleasure in writing and her puzzlement over the fact that so many of her friends (most of her class, in fact) dislike writing. Unlike her classmates, Shannon has not become a writing dropout.

Like other students who persist in writing despite the lack of support from their school program, Shannon has continued to experiment with her writing, enjoying the exploration of different story forms. Modeling her acknowledgments on what she has observed in stories she has read, Shannon was careful to include disclaimers regarding the authenticity of her story facts

The Pirate named Amy

Shannon M. Oct. 30

There once was a pirate her name was Amy. There once was a pirate captain his name was Sam. One day Amy wanted to ask Sam if she could be a pirate. Amy could not find him so she had to write a letter to 282-827-1-800-Address 228 Miland rive NEW Hamshier.

it said

Dear Captain Sam

I'm intrested in being a pirate. I have been in the pirateing bussens but I quit   Please return
Sinserly
to 288-West Av. Hiland Califernia ~

Dear

I resived your letter and I say yes. Meet me at the dook on North street. Captian what will happen? you decied

Sam

Figure 11.1 *Shannon's pirate story*

(see note to the left of the title in Figure 11.1). Also, she uses a rather sophisticated narrative technique, correspondence between characters, to recount her tale of adventure. When in doubt, Shannon resorts to letter-name spelling (senserly/sincerely; resived/received). And often, the letters are there but in the wrong order (Hampshier/Hampshire; captian/captain; decied/decide). Shannon demonstrates that she is not afraid to take risks in transcribing her story. Her primary focus is to get the meaning across, which she does admirably. Her freedom is enviable as is her creativity.

What needs to be remembered regarding the progress of youngsters who are transitional spellers is that to some extent the hard work has been done:

> Transitional spellers are readers. The source of the features, the generalizations about spelling they are beginning to manipulate, is in the print they see around them. The path to correct spelling lies through more reading, more writing, and more attention to the way words are put together. (Temple, Nathan, & Burris, 1982, p. 108)

Similar to Eric, Shannon's spelling substitutions reveal her struggle to come to terms with the abstractness of English orthography. Like most middle and upper elementary students, Shannon needs to continue to refine her spelling methods by becoming aware of semantic features of words, which dictate spelling processes. As Hodges (1981) puts it, there are two key word-building concepts that need to be a part of any spelling program: "First, words can be put to new uses by adding other words to them to form compound words; and, second, word elements (prefixes and suffixes) change the function or extend the meaning of root words" (p. 28). Exploring these aspects of words adds important spelling strategies to the young student's spelling repertoire. In addition to exploring word meanings and derivations, youngsters need to read, the most efficient method for gaining exposure to standard spellings of words, and to write regularly, preferably daily, so that they have opportunities to explore and try out their developing hypotheses related to spelling conventions.

RETHINKING SPELLING PROGRAMS

Spelling has a special place in the learning of transcription rules. Of all the subjects that fall into the category of language arts, the most time is devoted to the teaching of spelling. Yet, as any high school or college instructor can attest, a substantial proportion of students have not mastered the English spelling system. In my experience, college students who are having problems in writing tend to be in the transitional stage of spelling. Homophonic substitutions regularly appear in their writing, "illicit" for "elicit," for example, as well as vowel confusions resulting from a lack of awareness of how word derivations influence spelling patterns.

Reasons for the relatively widespread existence of this difficulty with spelling can be attributed to at least three sources: (1) lack of quantity and quality of reading; (2) lack of writing programs based on an understanding of the developmental nature of this kind of learning; and (3) spelling programs that overemphasize "sounding-out" or letter-name spelling strategies, which, if used exclusively, will lead youngsters astray.

More specifically, spelling programs need to be designed in ways that make sense in terms of how students learn. Beginning with the second or third grade, most elementary spelling programs go into high gear. At least 10 to 20 words are studied each week, and pretests are given at the beginning of the week and posttests at the end. In between, the words are used in sentences, put in alphabetical order, and written a given number of times. These approaches for exploring word spellings and meanings are limited at best and ineffective at worst. Spelling as a separate subject of study offers many more linguistically inventive and enriching possibilities than these examples. Some sensible guidelines should be considered in the design and implementation of elementary spelling programs:

1. *Spelling should be separated from composing.* A focus on spelling, or any other transcription rules, should never coincide with children's composing efforts until the youngsters have completed the stories and chosen to edit them—possibly for classroom publication and sharing.
2. *When exploring word meanings, the writing of sentences should be avoided.* To express the meaning of a word in a sentence is a contrived as well as difficult exercise. A good source for spelling words is a unit of study (social studies or science, for example), which provides a natural context for understanding word meanings. Another source is the words youngsters use frequently in their writing.
3. *Play involving word meanings (riddles, puns) and word structures (crossword puzzles, anagrams, palindromes) should form the heart of spelling practice.* These games provide a natural focus on letter sequences and/or meanings of words. As noted before, an excellent resource for these kinds of spelling activities is *Learning to Spell* by Richard Hodges (1981).
4. *Because English orthography is so dependent on word meanings, a focus on root words and derivations that influence spelling patterns is the most efficient method for helping youngsters move from transitional to conventional spelling.* Again, Hodges' (1981) pamphlet offers ways to explore these perspectives of spelling.

For transcription conventions, especially spelling, to become automatic, two things are required: first, regular exposure to print through reading, and second, ample opportunities to try out spelling rules through daily writing. Learning to spell, like learning to read and write, requires, above all, time to experiment with developing hypotheses regarding spelling rules.

The evidence of transitional spelling among adult writers is disturbing because it means that language learning has been short circuited. Conventional spelling is not desirable only because it is correct. Rather, spelling mastery reflects an appreciation of the diversity of the derivation of the English language and the network of semantic connections that link words to one another. Not to hold such a perspective of the language system is to be unaware and, therefore, unable to use the full power of this medium, especially in writing. It is, finally, the investigation of English in relation to the languages from which it was derived that lends a sense of depth and roots, indeed a sense of our social and cultural history, to our most important communication system. Similar to program suggestions for primary and elementary students, the only way to raise adult students' spelling consciousness is more reading, more writing (in which first drafts are not thought of as final papers), and more deliberate examination of the semantic relations that influence English spelling.

The lack of emphasis on writing programs in the primary grade curriculum has tended to leave a vacuum in this area. As a result, the implementing of writing workshops has met with relatively little resistance. Because there is no need to throw out the old to make room for the new, teachers and administrators have been willing to try process approaches to teaching writing. The initial resistance to allowing transcription errors to go uncorrected yields rather easily when teachers collect students' work over a period of time and see for themselves that these aspects of writing improve when youngsters read and write daily.

Based largely on the success of writing workshops, teachers and researchers are now taking on the task of redesigning elementary reading programs. The process approach to reading builds upon the elements described as central to the kindergarten reading program. In the next chapter we visit teachers in the primary grades who have moved from using basal reading materials to designing and implementing literature-based, reading process programs.

12

Building a Community of Readers

Independent-reading time had just begun in Elaine Iodice's first grade classroom. Students were called, table by table, to go to the class library and choose a book to read. The library consisted of an extensive collection of paperback and hardcover editions of children's storybooks. Many chose books by Paul Galdone, the author whose books were the current focus of the daily read-aloud sessions. Elaine had collected multiple copies of some of Galdone's folk and fairy tales from local libraries and displayed them prominently in the library area. With a book in hand, youngsters returned to their desks or found another spot in the room to read for the next 30 minutes. One girl stretched out on her stomach on the rug at the back of the room, with her book open in front of her. She was joined by two more girls, one lying parallel to her and the other placing herself at right angles to her two friends.

In addition to their reading books, the girls brought their notebooks (their reading logs) and their pencils. The questions to guide the reading had just been put on the board and read aloud: Does a character in your story remind you of anyone you know? Who? Why? When Elaine explained the questions she recalled a discussion the group had had when she had read a book in which one of the female characters reminded her of her mother. The three girls shifted arms, legs, and materials once more as they got comfortable and began to read. They knew that there would be a small group sharing time to discuss the reading questions before they wrote down their answers in their logs. The girls had already decided quietly that they would be in the same sharing group.

In this classroom, the first two hours of each morning are devoted to reading and writing. Within this time frame, there is a predictable sequence of activities and a balance between whole group, small group, and individual work times. Prior to the independent-reading time, there is a guided-reading session, a whole group activity in which the teacher provides the focus and chooses the content. Independent reading, including small group sharing, and the completing of the reading logs are followed by a writing workshop.

137

During the independent-reading time, Elaine moves around the room conferencing with children and keeping logs of her exchanges with each youngster.

Many of the children in this class had come from Diane Epstein's kindergarten or a kindergarten class in which there was a program similar to Diane's. At the beginning of the year, Elaine's program began more or less where the kindergarten program ended. At that time, the independent-reading time was simply a time to read on one's own. In the middle of the fall, reading logs were introduced. At that point, youngsters were asked simply to record the title and author of the book they read. Eventually, Elaine requested that log entries include a word or phrase that would indicate one of their reactions to what they read. In February, questions to guide the reading were introduced. These questions were similar to the ones recorded above in which the children were invited to make connections between the text and personal experiences. Questions that the youngsters were expected to respond to in their logs were introduced during read-aloud or guided-reading sessions. These elements of the program—independent reading, including conferencing; guided-reading sessions; and reading aloud by the teacher—shape the process approach to teaching reading. (See Chapter 9 for these elements as they relate to the kindergarten program.) Below, each aspect is described in detail and its particular strengths are underscored.

INDEPENDENT READING

Reading process programs are based on the premise that adults do not have to structure the reading time in order to control the pace, sequence, and variety of the students' exposure to reading materials. The premise is, rather, that students can be trusted as learners who want to grow as readers and can be allowed to choose their own reading material during independent-reading time.

It has been found, moreover, that student choice of reading materials tends to promote the growth of the vertical and horizontal aspects of the child's reading repertoire. The reading of materials in which youngsters function as "emergent" readers can be juxtaposed to the fluent reading of old favorites. Teachers often note how students will rise above their comfortable reading level and take on a book generally considered beyond their ability, because they are keenly interested in the topic. And just as young children love listening to their favorite stories read again and again, so young readers enjoy reading and rereading books of special interest to them.

The attitude of trusting the student's desire to learn has not been pervasive in our school system, especially in the primary years. In the past, placing so much responsibility for learning in the student's hands, while often considered useful for mainstream youngsters, was thought to be inappropriate for nonmainstream students. For the latter, it was believed that the highly structured, formal program typical of basal reading programs was necessary because these youngsters needed to be carefully and continually monitored. The fact that such programs place so little emphasis on teacher contact with individual students and, further, that they do not exploit student interest as a major factor in teaching reading has not deterred most school systems from using these programs as the exclusive approach for teaching reading to nonmainstream youngsters. Student difficulties with basal programs is cited as evidence that to expose these students to an independent-reading program would be foolish. Those difficulties are rarely considered as evidence that the source of the problem might rest with the design of the formal reading program.

As noted earlier, the major problem nonmainstream youngsters have when confronted with formal reading programs is that these approaches assume extensive knowledge of books and stories. In the primary years, these programs emphasize the teaching of print conventions, a meaningless focus for youngsters who are not already deeply engaged in the process of building their understanding of stories and their understanding of the functions of written language.

Nonmainstream youngsters are unable to respond to an independent-reading program that is not accompanied by daily read-aloud and guided-reading sessions. To repeat, there are three irreducible sides of the reading program triangle. Reading aloud by the teacher provides the needed conceptual foundations for understanding text structures. Guided-reading sessions, which may include shared-reading experiences, provide ongoing exposure to the content and form of written material. Together, these two frameworks provide the support needed for youngsters to become increasingly independent in their reading. From this point of view, it could be argued that nonmainstream youngsters need a process approach to reading more than their mainstream peers do, precisely because of its multifaceted design. Youngsters who come to school with limited experiences with literature need to connect in a personal way to written language, and this requires a program with the flexibility to exploit what they do know as a beginning point for building on what they don't know.

Reading Conferences

Reading process programs are often compared with individualized reading programs of the past in which students were allowed to choose their reading material. In these programs, teachers complained, with justification, that they were expected to function as tutors. A reading conference, in this design, tended to last about 20 minutes and required that the teacher monitor individual students' reading fluency, comprehension, and word analysis skills in nearly the same format as the reading lessons of basal programs. This meant that the teacher was engaged in a series of twenty-minute individualized teaching sessions, making it impossible to meet with more than two or three students each day. In this program, then, student choice of reading materials multiplied the time required to teach reading by the number of students in the class.

In the reading process program, the time the teacher spends with individuals is viewed differently. Conferencing is not tutoring. Rather, it is a time when teachers invite youngsters to share what they are reading. A strength of this program is that teachers allocate their time according to the needs of their students: Those who require more guidance can be given more time, while greater independence can be extended to those who are ready for it.

Organization

Many teachers prefer circulating among students, questioning, commenting, noting, and/or appreciating what each student is reading each day. They may even touch base with a student at the beginning of the period and get back to that youngster later on. They may meet with youngsters with similar difficulties as a group. Some teachers prefer to spend more time with each student and, therefore, have fewer conferences with each of their youngsters in any given time span. In many ways, the conference approach to teaching reading is similar in style and intent to the N–K teachers' approach to the class work time in which they move about the room aiding, questioning, and appreciating youngsters' explorations and activities. The teacher has the chance to individualize the approach because she or he can spend time with individual students, something that has been lacking in traditional reading programs. In fact, of all the things that appeal to teachers who have begun reading process programs, individual conferencing appears to be the aspect they find most satisfying as well as instructive. In contrast, formal reading programs tend to form a wall between teachers and students, rather than to provide a medium through which they can share thoughts and ideas. The time needed to get through the daily lessons in a formal program usually precludes the possibility of contact with individual students. The centerpiece of a reading process program, on the other hand, is the developing of a social relationship between teachers and their students in which understandings of literature and life are shared.

The teacher records salient aspects of individual conferences and uses these to plan small group and whole group sessions. This kind of documentation is an extension of the process approach to learning discussed in Chapter 7, in which teachers use the child's current views to guide them in the design of subsequent teaching/learning experiences. As weeks and months go by, the teacher's conference log provides the best resource for the assessment of student progress. Moreover, the discernment of patterns of difficulty, or particular interests, provides input for the design of read-aloud and guided-reading sessions.

Content

Just as I invited Christopher to share his thoughts about where snow comes from (see Chapter 7), so the teacher's first and most important conference goal is to invite children to share their thoughts and feelings about what they are reading. And just as Christopher revealed his then current views of the origins of snow, so children will reveal in what ways they are able to connect to texts and where they are confused. Again, the "yes, but . . ." followed by the teacher's explanation short circuits learning. Teachers must understand that the most generative approach to written language that they can model is that of reasoning about reading and about experiences, ideas, and feelings represented in print. Teachers must "try on" the child's viewpoint, that is, they must listen, really listen, as Lucy Calkins (1986) puts it, to what children are saying. What they hear will tell them how to respond.

The main focus of a literature-based reading program is to expose students to the world of fiction and the techniques as well as story structures or genres it employs to present its perspectives of imaginary places, people, and experiences. There are five key categories that guide conference exchanges related to literature:

1. Comprehension
   - Understanding the facts or literal meanings (Does the reader understand the progress of the narrative?)
   - Understanding implied meanings/logical inferences (Is the reader noting aspects of plot/character that must be inferred by reading between the lines?)

2. Life-to-text comparisons (Cochran-Smith, 1984)
   - Making sense of texts in terms of the reader's knowledge of the world and how it works (In *Are You My Mother?* [Eastman, 1960] that the baby bird could not fly because it was a baby is an inference the reader needs to make.)

3. Narrative forms and techniques (Moss, 1984)
   - Drawing attention to specific story genres (fairy tale, cumulative tale, mystery, and so forth)

- Drawing attention to the craft of fiction writing (thinking about uses of language to create a setting or define character, or thinking about narrative form, e.g., use of flashback, diary entries)

4. Text-to-text comparisons (Moss, 1984)
   - Discussing similarities between texts (Does this character remind you of a character in another book?)
   - Discussing differences between texts (How is this plot different from another plot that was discussed at an earlier time?)

5. Text-to-life comparisons (Cochran-Smith, 1984)
   - Juxtaposing fictionalized experiences and reader experiences (finding moments when "my experiences" are "just like the book")
   - Examining life perspectives and values represented by the text as similar to/different from the reader's experiences and views (for example, the question "Does a character in this book remind you of someone you know?" requires the reader to compare text descriptions and personal experience)

As described, these categories represent a very abstract framework for approaching literature. Given the context supplied by a particular story, however, it is relatively simple to make connections between text and talk. There is not necessarily a specific order in which these categories must be approached. The sequence of the conference exchange is largely determined by student response to the teacher's opening question/comment. Often, however, basic comprehension (category 1) of a particular plot or narrative must be established first, because making a match between reader understanding and text meanings deliberately set forth by the author provides the basis for discussion of the other categories. Moreover, comprehension discussions often involve category 2, because text meanings frequently can be explained only by drawing on the reader's general knowledge of the world. Understanding of narrative form and comparing texts are the main methods for expanding the reader's literary awareness (categories 3 and 4). Finally, evaluating material in terms of readers' specific life experiences underscores the value of literature as a way of defining what one thinks in relation to what others think (category 5).

Together, these approaches constitute a program for developing critical reading and thinking abilities, or the examination of the world of fiction as a reflection of life as we view it in our culture and our time. The process of reflecting on the origins of a book, of thinking about life values presented by a text, and of considering the extension and consequences of holding particular views and values must shape teacher–student conferences. This is the process by which reading becomes an extension of life experience as well as a crucial medium for building a rich and vital classroom community.

A GUIDED–READING SESSION

Below is a description of the guided-reading session designed and led by Lisa Goldstein, my student teacher working with Elaine. Like Donna in the kindergarten class, Lisa based her lesson on the model she had seen Elaine use with the class. Though it was only her fourth week in this classroom when I observed her lead this session and videotaped it, Lisa was thoroughly in tune with the children and the program. Her enthusiasm, as well as her delight in the give and take with the group, was very apparent.

Shared Reading

Lisa held up the book she was going to read. On the cover there was a picture of a bright orange pumpkin with the title, *The Pumpkin* (see Butler, 1984). She asked the group what they thought the story might be about. Most responded with the information that they had read the story before. So Lisa asked only those who hadn't read the story to respond to the question. This prompted two youngsters to tell quick pumpkin stories. Others were eager to give their hypothetical versions of this text (a common occurrence in this class) when Lisa uncovered a sheet of chart paper on which she had copied the text in large print. She directed the group to listen as she read:

Sister planted a pumpkin.	Mother picked the pumpkin.
Jimpkin, jumpkin, We'll all have pumpkin.	Jimpkin, jumpkin, We'll all have pumpkin.
Brother hoed the pumpkin.	I cut the pumpkin.
Jimpkin, jumpkin. We'll all have pumpkin.	Jimpkin, jumpkin, We all had pumpkin.
Father watered the pumpkin.	
Jimpkin, jumpkin. We'll all have pumpkin.	

As Lisa began the second round of repeated lines, it was difficult for most of the children to restrain themselves from joining in the reading. So Lisa encouraged them to read along with her.

Text and Print Patterns

After they finished, hands shot up in the air. The children were anticipating the next phase of the group session, in which they would be invited to point out examples of narrative form or print patterns. Individual students commented on the following aspects of the text:

1. Rhyming words (jimpkin, jumpkin, pumpkin)
2. Repetition (the two lines that rhyme)
3. *Have* to *had* (final line)
   - Lisa asked the child to clarify how the change of tense changed the meaning.
   - Lisa asked what else can show that something happened already (ed) and what that was called (suffix).
- Lisa asked what other suffix they remembered learning (ing).

4. *We'll* (a contraction)
   - Lisa asked youngsters to count the number of times it was repeated.
   - Lisa asked what it stands for.

No more hands were up, so Lisa suggested they read the story together again, which they did with energy and enthusiasm.

Storytime Talk

Lisa picked up the book and read it again, showing the pictures. Some joined the reading, but most scrutinized the pictures. The reading was followed by a discussion. Lisa's questions are shown below, with their categories indicated in the left column. She had an opening question and usually one or more follow-up questions in each category.

Comprehension.	What did they do at the end of the story?
Text-to-life.	Do you like pumpkin pie?
	Have you ever had pumpkin pie?
Narrative form.	What is the setting?
Life-to-text.	Can anyone tell me what kind of climate it is?
	Can you tell me what "climate" means?
Comprehension.	What does the pumpkin need to grow?
Text-to-life.	Do any of you have a garden?
	What do you grow in your garden?

Comprehension.	What did they do first?
Life-to-text.	Did they have to do it in that order?
	Why does it have to be done in that or-der?
	Why couldn't you water it before you plant it?
Comprehension.	Who worked on the pumpkin? (The whole family?)
Text-to-life.	Can you do other things as a whole fam-ily together?
	What fun things does your family do to-gether?
Life-to-text.	What holidays do we use pumpkins in?
	What can we do with pumpkins at these holidays?

Like Louise with her three-year-olds, Lisa models ways of looking at texts through the kinds of questions she asks. The simple plot did not require a great deal of exploration. Rather, Lisa used it as a jumping off point for making connections among life experiences and text descriptions (text-to-life). She focused attention on similarities between text situations and events in the children's lives (growing a garden, doing things as a family). At other moments, she integrated text ideas with other information students have about their physical and social worlds (life-to-text): specifically, with science (the planting sequence) and social studies (holidays in which pumpkins fig-ure prominently). Even this simple text, then, provided many opportunities to think about ways in which story meanings intersect with life experiences.

READING ALOUD: LITERATURE AND LIFE

For the last part of the session, Lisa read another book, *The Carrot Seed*, by Ruth Krauss (1945). This story, a classic in children's literature, is about a little boy who plants a carrot seed and waits patiently for it to come up. Day after day, he waters and weeds the garden, but nothing comes up. His dili-gence is made all the more poignant because family members tell him that nothing will come up. The boy continues to perform the watering and weed-ing tasks, and eventually the carrot does come up.

The group expressed pleasure in the story. The youngsters were especially impressed with the final illustration of a very large carrot. Lisa picked up the *The Pumpkin* and held it next to *The Carrot Seed*. She asked: "Can you tell me how these stories are the same?" This discussion was followed by a question about differences between the stories. In this discussion, the issue of sharing what was grown stimulated controversy among these first graders. In *The Pumpkin,* the entire family shared the work of raising the plant. According to many, since the boy in *The Carrot Seed* did all the work, he shouldn't have to share the results. Indeed, they were rather convincing in their defense of his right to eat the whole carrot himself because not only were the others of no help, but they continually expressed their doubts about it coming up at all. Others adopted the more socially acceptable view that the boy should share because people, especially families, *ought* to share with each other.

Lisa tended to be noncommittal in her response to this part of the discussion. She neither cut off nor stimulated the exchange. Controversies related to social behaviors frequently come up in classrooms in which discussions centering on literature as a reflection of life are a regular part of the program. Such exchanges should be encouraged because they represent the key method for developing critical reading. Story themes, by definition, pose particular views of life and thus they provide opportunities for listeners to dialogue with the author and among themselves about what these views are and how they are the same as or different from their ideas. Cochran-Smith (1984) defines this aspect of text-to-life considerations as "a kind of counseling vehicle" (p. 248). Because story events resemble life experiences, youngsters are prompted to discuss their feelings about similar situations in their lives. Often, children's views may not coincide with culturally accepted views of these situations. Cochran-Smith indicates that, at the nursery level, the expression of a diversity of views is usually accepted as beneficial. Adults tend to allow young children to express personal opinions without correcting them to conform to generally accepted social views.

As children move into the elementary grades, however, many teachers avoid or short circuit such discussions by stating generally accepted views as final conclusions. As youngsters mature, teachers appear to become more self-conscious about reinforcing "correct" social behaviors. Sharing, routines (obeying the rules), and expressing hostility (name-calling) are social issues that interest all school-age youngsters because they figure prominently in children's lives inside and outside of the classroom. Indeed, these are the issues that presented me with so many challenges when I taught three-year-olds (see Chapter 5).

School-age youngsters frequently hold views about these issues that may differ from accepted views. Like Christopher and the snow, youngsters reason from their life experiences. Their opinions of social behaviors derive from their observations of actions of the adults (mostly, parents and teachers) and peers with whom they have regular contact. Teachers must beware of the impulse to use discussions around these controversial issues as a time to indoctrinate youngsters in how they ought to behave—"Yes, we should all share, in families and in our classroom," and so forth. Such a response is similar to the "yes, but" reaction to children's misinterpretations of the workings of the physical world. This kind of adult response, as noted, tends to close off children's impulse to reason from experience, the most important response learners bring to the task of understanding the world around them.

To state a rule in absolute terms and in a way that is meant to cover all instances of one category of behavior (We must all share!) is meaningless. It has the ring of dogma and the "do-as-I-do-because-I-tell-you-to" message, which is antithetical to the development of critical thinking, a process that, by definition, invites exploration of different angles of an issue. As noted, the do-as-I-say approach characterized the nineteenth-century method for running a classroom community. The approach attempts to isolate intellectual growth from social understanding. In the process, critical thinking is undermined as a valued aspect of learning. Also, the attitude that such adult reactions model is the opposite of the message they are attempting to communicate.

Sharing, in this context, must begin with teachers' sharing—that is, really listening—to children's views. In literature discussions, to solicit youngsters' personal ideas, to ask for reasons for their views, and/or to guide them to think through consequences of particular actions are ways in which teachers can share by entering into children's perspectives of their world. In the social realm, the effort to articulate a particular view, to lay it out alongside other views, helps youngsters to understand the nature of their social world. Group controversy provides an ideal opportunity for discussing differing perspectives of living together, especially if these views are translated into common problems of classroom life. Discussions of differing views are especially useful because of the hypothetical nature of these exchanges. Everyone can try on different views of life, explore potential consequences, and compare one view with another within the safety of the classroom. The spirit of reflection is what most authors of fiction attempt to generate. The rich and extensive literature that the authors of children's stories have produced provides a vivid context within which even young children are stimulated to examine important ideas.

TOWARD A SCHOOL COMMUNITY

As I have watched the development of programs such as the ones described in this chapter, I have been struck by the energy and spirit with which both teachers and children approach their shared tasks of literacy teaching and learning. Choice and respect appear to be the elements that have contributed to the strength of this approach. Teachers are given choices regarding the shaping of their evolving programs. They take on pieces of the process approach to writing and reading in manageable bites. Teachers usually begin by implementing a writing workshop one year and then expand to include reading process the next. They may also choose, as Elaine has done, to include certain workbook materials as part of the reading/writing programs, in addition to the daily reading and writing process periods.

The commitment of the school's principal is essential to the successful development of this kind of program. In the school described above, the principal is committed to an independent-reading period for all classrooms and protects the two-hour time block teachers need for the leisurely and concentrated exploration of reading and writing. Moreover, he has welcomed the opportunity to collaborate in the writing project of a nearby college of education and to learn along with teachers and students. Over the past four years he has made it possible for interested teachers to work with trainers from the project and/or with other teachers in the school to develop their learning process programs. The principal also works closely with the district writing process coordinator, who, in addition to leading parent workshops and working regularly in the classrooms, acts as trainer, resource person, and collaborator with teachers in guiding the implementation of reading and writing process programs.

The assumption about education that underlies this approach is that social and intellectual experiences of life and learning are inextricably bound. Schools that have begun to adopt collaborative approaches to education are discovering that reading and writing are becoming more and more integrated with the rest of the curriculum, more and more driven by themes of special interest to individuals or an entire class group, and more and more prevalent in discussions among students and adults, because reading and writing represent some of the richest experiences of their lives. In short, over the course of a year, these classrooms become communities of people in which boundaries between teaching and learning tend to dissolve and to be replaced by collaborative exchanges among adults and children.

Epilogue

Shaping New Images
of Literacy Education

Each semester, I have the students in my reading course write a series of personal memory papers in which they describe their experiences related to literacy learning. My goal is to find a way to connect students' personal experiences to course content. I have found over the years that memories of reading and writing can be a powerful source of inspiration for beginning teachers to rethink traditional literacy programs. Typically, I devote a portion of four out of fourteen class meetings to reading and discussing experiences described in these papers. The impact of these sessions builds during the semester. Not only do students begin to look forward to these sharing sessions, but listening to one another's papers stimulates everyone's memories. Childhood experiences around reading and writing are remembered and relived. They provide a very human perspective to our theoretical discussions. Highlights of dialogues stimulated by the sharing of excerpts from student papers in a recent class group are described below.

FAMILIES AND STORIES

The first memory paper is due the second class session. The assignment is loosely described as writing about memories of learning to read in or out of school. The most important guideline, I tell students, is to find vivid experiences to write about.

The first sharing session, then, occurs during our third class session. I have read the papers, chosen the excerpts I want to read, and organized the sequence of the readings. I could approach these sessions differently, by having students gather in small groups and share their thoughts and experiences more informally. I do use this method at other points in the course. With these papers, though, I jealously guard the leadership role. It is a way of building a set of shared experiences related to literacy learning in a class of 25 students. Further, hearing about one another's memories promotes the awareness that, despite differences in age and background, we share similar feelings and experiences related to reading and writing.

I open our first memory session with the following excerpt from Susan Devane's paper:

> One of my earliest memories is of my grandfather reading to me and tell-ing me stories. Every weekday, he would come to our house for his din-ner, which was eaten at midday, and after the meal, when my father had returned to work and my mother was washing the dishes, he would settle into the high-backed wing chair and storytime would begin. Sometimes other children from the street would join us, but I always got to sit next to him. My favorite stories were the ones my grandad would make up. I believed every word. In particular, I remember how he told of the time when he was on a boat to China when the engines failed in a storm. My grandad jumped over the side of the boat and swam the rest of the way to China pulling the boat with the anchor chain between his teeth.

After the reading, I ask Susan to tell us more about her memories of her grandfather. Raised in England, Susan describes how her grandfather was a favorite among the kids of her block, who would often come to the door and ask if "Grandad could come and play."

Susan's paper is followed by my reading excerpts from Riva Bennet's and Susan D'Alessio's papers, which describe the hearing of stories at bedtime as favorite moments each of them shared with an older sister and their father. In both these families, the ritual was that the sisters would get ready for bed, snuggle next to their father, one on either side, and listen as stories were read or told. What comes through is the warmth and love that Riva and Susan associate with these early reading experiences. The point is made, and made eloquently, that learning to read is basically a social experience. Those few papers in which students recall disliking reading in their early years tend to be from those who do not have any memories, or any pleasant memories, of reading with members of their family.

I turn to Susan Devane's paper again and read another paragraph describing some of her early school experiences.

> Our teachers were kindly women for the most part but our headmaster was a sadistic tyrant, who terrorized both teachers and students. He would periodically come into our classroom and ask to hear us read. The teacher would try to protect us by calling upon the best readers but often

[he] would pick out a child himself. What agony that was to listen to our classmate stumbling over the words, becoming more and more nervous, as we all waited for the tirade that inevitably followed. Often the reading lesson ended with one child or another being strapped on the hands with a leather belt. I hate that man to this day.

This memory of anguished moments associated with learning to read is supported by the sharing of fears about reading in front of the class. Though no one else remembers corporal punishment being a part of their school experiences, all remember humiliations experienced either directly or, when witnessing a classmate in trouble, vicariously. The consensus we reach is that the classroom is all too often a source of unnecessary anguish and embarrassment for many students. To balance the picture, memories of pride and a sense of accomplishment related to school reading tasks are recalled and discussed. The overriding sense is that classroom reading experiences are extremely significant as well as instructive. We agree that students learn as much or more from how something is taught as from what is taught.

Nearly all of the students report that in their early childhood years a particular book held a special fascination. With this particular class, many of the women mention *Madeline* (Bemelmans, 1977) as being an early favorite. The Barbar series (DeBrunhoff, 1961) and *Curious George* (Rey, 1969) also rank among the best loved picture books of this group. We decide that the character Madeline, like Curious George, appeals because she is spunky and mischievous, traits not often found (until recently) in books in which the central character is a little girl.

The sharing of these episodes lends weight to the significance of reading to young children. The stage is set for the regular recall of anecdotes as a way of adding personal significance to our theoretical discussions. The idea of learning from each other and about each other begins to gain momentum as a useful source of information for becoming a teacher.

CURRENT PRACTICE IN PERSPECTIVE

About midway through the semester, we reach the point when it is time to evaluate basal reading materials. I do not attempt to present an unprejudiced perspective of these programs. By this time, the students are able to distinguish between formal and informal methods of teaching and are well aware of my preference for the latter. During these sessions, the difficulty I have is allowing the evaluation to proceed without feeling that I must put my stamp on what students think and say every step of the way. In short, the challenge, similar to that of teaching young children, is to remember that I am there to provide experiences from which students can learn rather than to articulate perspectives that they are asked to imitate.

This class, like most others, arrives at a point when the students begin to feel that basal materials have a place in the reading curriculum. To all of us, the reading lesson format has the ring of school. Rereading these materials revives memories of mornings spent following this predictable sequence of activities. The review exercises at the beginning of the lesson, the page-by-page reading of the story, and the workbook sheets to be completed on one's own are all very familiar. Moreover, when examined from an adult perspective, they provide a very definable shape to the job of teaching reading.

The sense of security that the carefully outlined reading lessons provide cannot be overlooked. Students are becoming keenly aware of the complexities of the teaching task, and they see the benefits of having program materials that outline daily activities. I remind them that these materials can function very nicely as a guide. I suggest that they must beware of the temptation to use the materials as a prescription or recipe that is followed each day and comes to represent the entire reading program. The students are usually quick to pick up the demeaning quality of the teacher manuals. Moreover, they are critical of the repetitiousness of the lessons and the undue emphasis on workbook materials.

Gradually, the students articulate what they feel is a reasonable approach to reading programs in the primary years. The reading lesson format, they note, has the potential to be revised and extended to include shared-book experiences and story discussions. Furthermore, reading aloud by the teacher and independent-reading time can be built around the daily guided-reading lessons. Having resolved for the moment the conflict between current practices and new perspectives of learning to read, the group is ready to turn to the final phase of course work.

READING WITH THE HEART

The rest of the class sessions are spent discussing the design of literature-based reading programs for the primary grades. A good place to begin is to discuss the power of the experience of reading a good book. I ask that they write a paper describing a memorable experience related to reading a particular book.

I open the sharing session by reading Judy Knoop's description of her experience with *The Exorcist* by William P. Blatty (1971). Judy takes us back to her seventeenth summer and the weekend in which her friends had agreed to go, on Sunday evening, to the movie based on the book. Determined to finish the book (with 200 pages to go) before seeing the movie, she stayed up most of Saturday night reading. At 5 A.M., she reports that her courage was "running out" and she decided to go to bed and finish the last pages in the morning when "the sun would be up and so would my brother." She set the alarm for 7:30.

> It seemed as if minutes had passed when I was awakened by the blaring alarm. Daylight had taken the jelly out of my legs and the pounding from my heart. I finished the book with a sense of satisfaction and also one of loss. The loss is how one feels after reading a good book, having been in another place with intriguing people and vivid surroundings.

The idea of a good book evoking a sense of loss after it is completed strikes a chord among other members of the class. The loss, we decide, is due in part to the sense of total immersion that we experience when reading a good book. Many in the class wrote about having spent, at times in their lives, many long hours on the crowded, noisy New York subways. The experience, they report, is totally transformed by using the time for reading. "You are literally removed from your surroundings," comments Jaime Maniatis, who also reports that she has missed subway stops countless times because she was immersed in a book.

Reading, we conclude, more than any other vicarious experience, gives us the sense that we are not just observing, but actually participating in, the lives of others. Someone comments that it is the identification with a particular character that blurs the divisions between fantasy and reality. Alyssa Bellis reports that, at times, she experiences confusion about whether she has read something in a book or whether it has actually happened.

Another chord in this class of mostly women is sounded when I read excerpts from Beth Beilin's paper. Beth begins her paper by saying that it didn't take long to remember a vivid experience with a particular book. What made her hesitate to use it in her paper was the nature of the book. Fortunately, the vividness of her memory overcame her hesitations. She went to the closet in which she kept a shopping bag of old paperbacks and pulled out the one that had evoked these memories.

> My eyes study the now yellowing images portrayed: two figures sentimentally locked, eternally, in a loving embrace; the title boldly printed beneath. "Passionate! Tumultuous! Inevitable! *Sweet Savage Love.* Rosemary Rogers' resplendent saga of beautiful, flame-haired Virginia Brandon and her undying love for Steven Morgan, the handsome, hard-faced renegade who steals her innocence and her heart. . . ." Within the rapturous realm of Steve and Ginny's sultry story, my 13-year-old romantic visions found a place to take root and flower.

Before I began reading this excerpt I assured Beth that her sentiments are shared by others in the class who included similar descriptions in their papers. After the reading, however, the numbers of emphatic listeners doubled as others recounted intense, adolescent experiences with romantic novels. I then read the end of Beth's paper in which she describes her adult view of those years and those books.

> In the years to follow, my infatuation with the historical romance genre persisted. An endless row of repetitious titles ensued . . . until a certain impatience with the monotonous format led me to appreciate a more mature and refined style. But I owe an invaluable debt of gratitude to those two immortal lovers, Steve and Ginny, for together they opened my heart and my mind to the wondrous possibilities confined to the boundaries of a book.

Kevin Gutterman writes of a similar time in life. The story that provided much solace during his teenage years is Ray Bradbury's *Dandelion Wine* (1982). Kevin reports that he remembered being thrilled to discover a character so much like himself.

> How could [Bradbury] have created a character so much like me that I wanted to pull him from the pages of my book, give him a big hug and shout, "Yes, I understand what you are going through. I know! I know!"?

Kevin goes on to describe how the memory of the story brings back memories of the actual book: "how [it] felt in my hands, the size of the words on the page, and the pleasant smell that all paperback books seem to have." Such memories, we agree, contribute to the lasting impact of certain books. We take with us not just the people and places in the book, but also times, places, and sensations related to the reading experience.

I turned to Susan Devane's description of one of her memorable reading experiences at the end of this session. Susan reports that when she was 14 *Pride and Prejudice* by Jane Austen (1813/1984) was assigned in school. She recalls that she enjoyed this book and others by Austen, which she sought out on her own. She concludes, however, that though Austen's "gentle humor and ladylike heroines were pleasing [they] were just not relevant to my own life." Subsequently, her class was assigned *Wuthering Heights* by Emily Bronte (1847/1985). Though she expected more of the same, she reports that the experience turned out to be very different.

> The setting was instantly recognizable. I had spent some time on the Yorkshire Moors and [apparently] the moors of Northumberland were

just as wild and beautiful. My father often would take us exploring on the moors on Sunday. I had seen first-hand how a sunny day could change in the blink of an eye. A sudden squall would sometimes sweep across the moors, sending us scattering back to the car. I particularly remember one day [when] our car [broke] down miles from anywhere. A passing motorist picked up my father to take him to a telephone to call for help, but my mother, sister, and I waited with the car. We were there for hours and the moors became a very frightening, eerie place as dusk began to fall. I usually didn't like descriptive passages in a book and tended to skip over them to get to the action, but Bronte's descriptions I loved. "Yes, that's just what it's like," I thought.

To me, Heathcliff and Catherine fit perfectly into these surroundings. Their passionate and stormy relationship seemed bred of the moors. Being a teenager with my own black moods and despairs, I empathized greatly with the characters, something I had never experienced before in a book. In my mind's eye I pictured Heathcliff to look like Elvis Presley, with whom I was hopelessly in love.

The ease and eloquence with which Susan wrote about her experiences are appreciated by the group. Only a few of us in this class were old enough to share Susan's romantic vision of Elvis Presley. Having read *Wuthering Heights* at a similar point in my life, I remember substituting the image of my then current romantic hero, Marlon Brando, for the moody and mysterious Heathcliff. Like Beth, Susan ends her paper with a paragraph that lends an adult perspective to these experiences.

Until I read *Wuthering Heights* I had enjoyed books, but did not realize the powerful portraits that could be drawn with the pen. I came away from that book with a new awe at the power of words and a yardstick with which to measure my future reading. It has been many years since I read *Wuthering Heights*. Is it as wonderful as I remember it? I think I'll read it again.

The discussion that follows the reading of Susan's final paragraph leads us to consider or, rather, reconsider the long-range significance of reading. We decide that a main goal of a reading program should be to aid the child's development of a vivid and lasting relationship to literature. The quantity of available books for young children and the pleasure of the experience of sharing stories give support to the idea that reading and learning to read can be pleasurable and riveting events both in and out of school.

During the last class session, students begin to express their ideas in ways that indicate that they are intrigued by the possibilities of teaching collaboratively and of creating a classroom community in which experiences with literature are shared regularly. We recognize that there is a gap between their experiences in this course and the designing and implementing of innovative literacy programs for 25 children. But they are on their way. Most have become authorities in their circle of family and friends; they buy books for nieces and nephews and are regular demonstrators of informal read-aloud sessions.

I leave them with the idea that the revolutionizing of reading programs is largely in the hands of teachers. It is teachers who are in the classroom everyday, working with children. It is teachers who are in charge of what goes on in their classrooms and who are ultimately the best judge of what kinds of experiences their students need. It is teachers who can and must become a significant source for the continuing research and development of sensible and meaningful programs for young children. It is, finally, teachers working together and learning from each other who can make a difference in how we teach and what we teach, a difference that can result in a population of youngsters who are on their way to a lifetime of satisfying experiences with reading and writing.

REFERENCES

INDEX

ABOUT THE AUTHOR

References

Austen, J. (1813/1984). *Pride and prejudice*. New York: Grosset and Dunlop.

Baghban, M. (1984). *Our daughter learns to read and write: A case study birth to three*. Newark, DE: International Reading Association.

Bemelmans, L. (1977). *Madeline*. Auckland, New Zealand: Puffin Books.

Blatty, W. (1971). *The exorcist*. New York: Harper and Row.

Bradbury, R. (1982). *Dandelion wine*. New York: Bantam Books.

Bronte, E. (1847/1985). *Wuthering heights*. New York: Penguin Books.

Bruner, J. (1983). *Child's talk: Learning to use language*. New York: W. W. Norton.

Butler, A. (1984). *The story box in the classroom: Stage 1*. San Diego, CA: Wright Group.

Calkins, L. (1983). *Lessons from a child*. Portsmouth, NH: Heinemann Educational Books.

———. (1986). *The art of teaching writing*. Portsmouth, NH: Heinemann Educational Books.

Clay, M. M. (1975). *What did I write?* Portsmouth, NH: Heinemann Educational Books.

Cochran-Smith, M. (1984). *The making of a reader*. Norwood, NJ: Ablex Publishing.

———. (1986). Reading to children: A model for understanding texts. In B. B. Schiefflin & P. Gilmore (Eds.), *The acquisition of literacy: Ethnographic perspectives* (pp. 35–54). Norwood, NJ: Ablex Publishing.

Cochrane, O., Cochrane, D., Scalena, S., & Buchanan, E. (1984). *Reading, writing and caring*. New York: Richard C. Owen Publishers.

Cuban, L. (1984). *How teachers taught*. New York: Longman Publishers.

DeBrunhoff, J. (1961). *The story of Barbar*. New York: Random House.

Dore, J., Franklin, M. B., Miller, R. T., & Ramer, A. L. H. (1976). Transitional phenomena in early language acquisition. *Journal of Child Language 3*, 343–50.

Eastman, P. D. (1960). *Are you my mother?* New York: Random House.

Fortney, F. (n.d.) Personal communication.

Galda, L. (1984). Narrative competence: Play, storytelling, and story comprehension. In A. Pelligrini & T. Yawkey (Eds.), *The development of oral and written language in social contexts* (pp. 105–18). Norwood, NJ: Ablex Publishing.

Genishi, C., & Dyson, A. H. (1984). *Language assessment in the early years*. Norwood, NJ: Ablex Publishing.

Gibson-Geller, L. (1985). *Word play and language learning for children.* Urbana, IL: National Council of Teachers of English.

Gleason, J. B. (1967). Do children imitate? Paper read at International Conference on Oral Education of the Deaf, Lexington School for the Deaf. New York City.

Goodman, K. (1986). *What's whole in whole language?.* Portsmouth, NH: Heinemann Educational Books.

Graves, D. H. (1983). *Writing: Teachers and children at work.* Portsmouth, NH: Heinemann Educational Books.

Hansen, J. (1987). *When writers read.* Portsmouth, NH: Heinemann Educational Publishers.

Harste, J. C., Burke, C. L., & Woodward, V. A. (1984). *Language stories and literacy lessons.* Portsmouth, NH: Heinemann Educational Books.

Heath, S. B. (1983). *Ways with words: Language, life, and work in communities and classrooms.* New York: Cambridge University Press.

Hodges, R. E. (1981). *Learning to spell.* Urbana, IL: National Council of Teachers of English.

Holdaway, D. (1979). *The foundations of literacy.* New York: Scholastic.

———. (1984). *Stability and change in literacy learning.* Portsmouth, NH: Heinemann Educational Books.

Hornsby, D., & Sukarna, D., with Parry, J. (1986). *Read on—A conference approach to reading.* Portsmouth, NH: Heinemann Educational Publishers.

Johnson, T. D., & Louis, D. R. (1987). *Literacy through literature.* Portsmouth, NH: Heinemann Educational Publishers.

Krauss, R. (1945). *The carrot seed.* New York: Harper & Row.

Moss, J. (1984). *Focus units in literature: A handbook for elementary teachers.* Urbana, IL: National Council of Teachers of English.

Newkirk, T., & Atwell, N. (Eds.) (1982). *Understanding writing.* Chelmsford, MA: The Northeast Regional Exchange, Inc.

Newman, J. M. (Ed.) (1985). *Whole language: Theory in use.* Portsmouth, NH: Heinemann Educational Books.

Paley, V. G. (1986). *Mollie is three.* Chicago, IL: The University of Chicago Press.

Pelligrini, A., & Yawkey, T. (Eds.) (1984). *The development of oral and written language in social contexts.* Norwood, NJ: Ablex Publishing.

Piaget, J. (1973). *To understand is to invent: The future of education.* New York: Grossman Publishers.

Pease, D., & Gleason, J. B. (1985). Gaining meaning: Semantic development. In J. B. Gleason (Ed.), *The development of language* (pp. 103–38). Columbus, OH: Charles E. Merrill Publishing.

Popular education. (1826, July 12). *Hampshire Gazette,* p. 1.

Read, C. (1975). *Children's categorization of speech sounds in English.* Urbana, IL: National Council of Teachers of English.

Reading in junior classes. (1985). New York: Richard C. Owen Publishers.

Rey, H. A. (1969). *Curious George.* Boston, MA: Houghton Mifflin.

Rice, J. (1892/1969). *The public school system of the United States.* New York: Arno Press.

Rogers, R. (1974). *Sweet savage love.* New York: Avon Books.

Schmidt, W. (1987, July 9). Paddling in school: Custom under fire anew. *New York Times,* pp. A1, A22.

Schwartz, J. I. (1988). *Encouraging early literacy.* Portsmouth, NH: Heinemann Educational Books.

Snow, C., & Ninio, A. (1986). The contracts of literacy: What children learn from learning to read books. In W. H. Teale & E. Sulzby (Eds.), *Emergent literacy* (pp. 116–38). Norwood, NJ: Ablex Publishing.

Sulzby, E., & Teale, W. H. (1985). Writing development in early childhood. *Educational Horizons 64,* 8–11.

Taylor, D. (1983). *Family literacy: Young children learning to read and write.* Portsmouth, NH: Heinemann Educational Books.

Teale, W. H. (1984). Reading to young children: Its significance for literacy development. In H. Goelman, A. A. Oberg, & F. Smith (Eds.), *Awakening to literacy* (pp. 110–21). Portsmouth, NH: Heinemann Educational Books.

———. (1986). Home background and young children's literacy development. In W. H. Teale & E. Sulzby (Eds.), *Emergent literacy* (pp. 173–206). Norwood, NJ: Ablex Publishing.

Teale, W. H., & Sulzby, E. (1986). Introduction: Emergent literacy as a perspective for examining how young children become writers and readers. In W. H. Teale & E. Sulzby (Eds.), *Emergent literacy* (pp. vii–xxv). Norwood, NJ: Ablex Publishing.

Temple, C. A., Nathan, R. G., & Burris, N. A. (1982). *The beginnings of writing.* Boston, MA: Allyn and Bacon.

Weber, E. (1984). *Ideas influencing early childhood education.* New York: Teachers College Press.

Wells, G. (1986). *The meaning makers: Children learning language and using language to learn.* Portsmouth, NH: Heinemann Educational Books.

Index

Nonmainstream youngsters, 73, 120, 121, 138–39

One-on-one interactions, 10, 55
Orange books, 108

Paley, Vivian Gussin, 50–53, 60
Paragraph formation, 131
Parents. *See* Caregivers; Family life
Patterned text, 18–19, 103
Patterns, writing, 91–92
Peers. *See* Friendship; Sociability
Phonemes, 93, 94, 95, 105
Phonemic spelling, 94, 108
Phonics, 13, 119
Piaget, Jean, 78, 80–81
Picture books, 9–10, 16, 54, 69, 109, 151
Play, 6–8, 47–49
Play-Doh, 49–50
Pleasure of reading, 24, 73, 119, 121, 123, 155
Plot machinery, 67–69
Primary grades, 115–25
Principal, 148
Print
  conventions, 104, 139
  and early education, 31
  and emergent literacy, 25–32
  and family life, 25–28
  forms, 27, 31
  functions, 25–28, 31
  patterns, 96–97, 121, 144
  practice, 87–92
  and routine, 25
  rules, 121
  sharing, 104
  and social networks, 25
  and sounds, 93, 94
  and speech, 105
  symbols, 93
  and voice match, 121–22

words in, 104
  See also Reading; Writing; *name of specific topic*
Process approach, 127–31, 136, 139–41, 148
Punctuation, 129–30, 131
Puppet theatre, 106

Quantity of reading material, 110
Questions, 63, 72, 81, 129, 137, 138, 144–45

Read-along activities, 107
Reading
  and building a community of readers, 137–48
  children's repertoire for, 109–11
  comprehension, 120, 121, 139–40, 141, 144–45
  definition of, 13, 21, 23–24
  failure rate of schools in teaching, 13–14
  and familiarity with subject matter, 99–100
  fears of, 150–51
  with the heart, 152–56
  rate of, 110
  and stages of learning, 14, 24
  as a vicarious experience, 152–56
  See also name of specific topic
Reading aloud, 100–102, 119, 121, 129–30, 138, 139, 141, 143, 145–47, 152
Reading logs, 137–38
Read-the-room, 107
Real world. *See* Fiction and the real world
Recognition scene, 69–71
Repetition
  and basal readers, 123, 152
  and elementary education, 119, 123
  and emergent literacy/readers, 18–19, 23, 109

About the Author

Linda Gibson has been a teacher and observer of young children for over 20 years. A specialist in early childhood education and children's language development, she has spent 15 years as a teacher and researcher in classrooms of three- through seven-year-olds. She is the author of *Word Play and Language Learning for Children,* a book that explores the integration of children's verbal play with language programs in nursery and elementary classrooms. As an undergraduate at Connecticut College, she majored in History of Art. She received her masters degree in early childhood education from Bank Street College, and completed her Ed.D. at New York University. Currently, she is an associate professor in the School of Education at Queens College, City University of New York.